SPARK
FOR THE
FIRE

SPARK

FOR THE

FIRE

How youthful thinking
unlocks creativity

IAN WHARTON

Hh

HARRIMAN HOUSE LTD
3A Penns Road
Petersfield
Hampshire
GU32 2EW
GREAT BRITAIN
Tel: +44 (0)1730 233870

Email: enquiries@harriman-house.com
Website: www.harriman-house.com

First published in Great Britain in 2013.
Copyright © Ian Wharton.

ISBN: 9780857193469

British Library Cataloguing in Publication Data
A CIP catalogue record for this book can be obtained from the British Library.

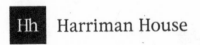

Every paperback copy of *Spark for the Fire* comes with a free download of the eBook
edition. Head to **ebooks.harriman-house.com/sparkforthefire** to grab yours.

For my parents Alan and Rita, and my big sister Helen
– Thank you for 28 years of saying "You can do it, kid"

ABOUT THE AUTHOR

Ian Wharton is a creative director at the global ideas and innovation agency AKQA. Previously a partner at tech start-up Zolmo, Ian led the creative for the Apple Design Award-winning apps for Jamie Oliver, some of the top-rated, top-grossing apps for iPhone and iPad with over 9 million downloads. During that time, Zolmo was ranked in *Design Week*'s Top 50 Design Consultancies.

After graduating best-of-show from university with short animated film *Solar* (2007), earning a Royal Television Society Award, Ian joined visual effects company The Mill as an art director. There he designed commercials for Audi and EA and game trailers for Sony. Ian has since been named an Art Directors Club 'Young Gun' and one of BIMA's Digital Hot 100.

As a regular speaker on creativity and the mobile industry, Ian contributed to the no.1 best-selling *App & Mobile Case Study Book* (2011), serves as digital jury foreman for the D&AD Student Awards, and mentors at London's School of Communication Arts.

FEATURING

AJAZ AHMED
Founder and CEO, AKQA

ADAM BIRD
Director, McKinsey & Company

PAUL BRAZIER
Executive creative director, AMV BBDO

TIM BROWN
CEO, IDEO

TIM LINDSAY
CEO, D&AD

MILLS
Co-founder, ustwo

JEAN OELWANG
CEO, Virgin Unite

JAMIE OLIVER
Chef and campaigner

NICK PARK
Creator, Wallace & Gromit
Academy Award-winner

LORD DAVID PUTTNAM
Chancellor, Open University
Academy Award-winner

EMMA SEXTON
Director, SheSays

RORY SUTHERLAND
Vice-chairman, Ogilvy Group UK
Former president, IPA

MICHAEL WOLFF
Co-founder, Wolff Olins

FOREWORD

Ajaz Ahmed
Founder and CEO of AKQA

I usually put much more emphasis on the present than the past but for this foreword I want to go back in time, to share some history and a glimpse of my youth.

Fourteen years old and still at school, a few classmates and I were huddled around a long wooden table. We were finding creative ways to make the minutes pass until the next bell sounded for home time. The art teacher came round to look over our shoulders. Knowing his glare was about to fall on my blank sheet, I started to draw.

I had no idea what I was going to draw – I just let my imagination take control. Musicians talk about being 'lost in music' and in that moment I think I understood what they meant. The image being produced, by some unknown power in my subconscious, mesmerised our teacher. I moved the drawing closer so he could get a better look. He peered at it, muttered, "That's not the idea of a 14-year-old," and walked off.

Two years later, aged 16, I entered a creative competition sponsored by the government and a leading design magazine. The brief was to create an anti-smoking ad campaign aimed at young people. I put together a portfolio of ideas, sent it in and heard nothing back. A brief period of time passed, the magazine issue with the winner in appeared and unfortunately my work had not been victorious. But around six months later, the government's official ad campaign launched in magazines and on billboards with what looked exactly like my work and ideas. Only, I didn't get paid. I didn't even get a credit.

Aged 20, and recognising the internet as the most profound of revolutions, I decided I didn't want to miss out on its possibilities. I decided to start my own web-based business. I approached the managing director of an agency that had been a supplier to a corporation I had worked with during summer holidays as a teenager. I asked if I could start my company in an unused corner of his office. Instead of paying him rent, he could have the company. I thought it was a pretty generous deal; I just wanted to get started. He told me that it wouldn't be possible and added: "Listen, you'll probably fail, but at least you're doing something none of your mates at university are doing."

It's impossible to separate an entrepreneur from his dreams. And from these experiences I learned three things. First, that not everyone in authority is a role model, nor will they always encourage you or play fair. Second, it's important to have heroes who transcend the people you may come across day-to-day. And third, that external forces do not control your destiny. You do.

Going through these experiences as a kid taught me that it's important to encourage youthful energy, not hold it back. One of the many great gifts of being young is that we think we can achieve anything. The only problem is that such a gift can be fragile: sometimes when we share our dreams with certain kinds of people – teachers, bosses, others in authority – their reactions suffocate our imagination and kill the creative spirit. But it's important not to let that happen: such self-belief also explains why young entrepreneurs make their businesses a canvas for their imagination, a new kind of playground, a more exciting kind of company.

That's certainly what my business – AKQA – has always been for me. I started it aged 21. We now employ 1,500 people in 11 offices around the world, working as a digital agency with clients such as Nike, Red Bull, Audi and Google. Our business has been able to thrive because of a few simple and enduring principles: a firm belief in the virtuous circle – if you do good work, it will lead to other things – and in the constant need for reinvention in order to stay relevant.

From day one our mission has been: 'the future inspires us, we work to inspire'. And when we talk about 'the future' we don't just mean the work that we are creating. We are also talking about the next generation of talent. We want to be a company that encourages creativity and experimentation because it's in our DNA – it is the lifeblood that keeps the company innovating and reaching for the impossible.

Today, the most exciting part of my job is the incredible number of artists, storytellers and innovators I get to work with. Ian Wharton is a creative entrepreneur with a passion for excellence. He has won numerous awards for his work across many disciplines and has already made his mark with a body of work that is beautifully crafted, elegant and inspirational. He represents a new generation of thinkers who see no boundaries to achieving their dreams. This book is a celebration of them and of the most powerful force in the universe: imagination.

Ajaz Ahmed

CONTENTS

Creativity is for the
bright-eyed and bushy-tailed

INTRODUCTION

This is an extraordinary time for people with a desire to make things.

Everyone has the power to broadcast, publish or distribute whatever their imaginations conceive. Technology is making creativity more accessible – products can get to market easier, stories can be told to more people and businesses can be built quicker. If you have an idea for an audience, there is nothing, *absolutely nothing*, to stop you from reaching them.

Sixty years ago, to reach their audience, a filmmaker required expensive and complex camera equipment, reels of 35mm film – of which 1,000 feet provided 11 minutes of footage – and a lab to process and cut the negative to be shipped to theatres worldwide.

Today the modest tools required are a digital camera, a laptop and some consumer software at a fraction of the cost. And successful feature films have been made with little more.

But technology, for all its benefits, is an equal distraction. Our obsession with hardware and software innovation makes it easy for the important things to be overlooked. Technology aside, much of what was true for the filmmaker then is true now. Circumstances are as uncertain. We have a culture in constant flux and young people who are living their lives just as differently to those of previous generations. They are finding their entertainment, products and services through increasingly evolving means. They do not care about the definitions of platforms or devices which creators spend too much time deliberating, they care *only* about the content.

The way to move things forward cannot lie in technology alone. It must ultimately rest, as it always has done, on *creativity*. What counts is having meaningful ideas and timeless stories to share that are worthy of the investment of people's time. Creativity and its potential to react to change provides an opportunity for all the rules to be broken – happily, just when the rules themselves are getting in the way.

When film studios in the 1950s needed a way to fill emptying seats due to the rapid growth of television, the best of them were willing to experiment and invest in big new productions. As a result the decade gave birth to two innovations. One was the original incarnation of 3D cinematography, a technology gimmick that passed as quickly as it surfaced (until recently). The other was to look to radical new stories and genres, a way to flex the framework of audience expectation and catch them off guard. This produced the golden age of cinematic sci-fi, with films such as *The War of the Worlds* (1953) and *20,000 Leagues Under the Sea* (1954). Not to mention the rewards from other genres with the likes of *Ben-Hur* (1959) and Hitchcock's *Rear Window* (1954).

Today, the world is still up for grabs for people who are willing to unleash their creative potential regardless of platform or technology. On 4 February 2004, a 19-year-old Harvard sophomore started a website from his dorm room with a handful of friends. I could probably stop there. You already know this story. The site was the beginnings of Facebook, and that student has since been glorified and vilified, immortalised (to some degree) by Hollywood, connected over a tenth of the global population and is someone who has perhaps forever changed the world and the way we live our lives. In 2010 he was named 'Person of the Year' by *TIME* magazine and after the Initial Public Offering of his company in 2012 he became the 29th-richest person on the planet.

Mark Zuckerberg has achieved all this and, at the time of writing, he is still only 29 years old. So he's doing OK. His story and those like it is partially what this book is dedicated to. By conventional definitions, Zuckerberg and his team had zero experience and followed little etiquette, yet what they created shows that unquestioned youthful ability, belief, creative potential and daring exploration with a disruptive idea can lead to something game-changing.

Over the past ten years I have met and worked with some of the world's most established creatives, brands and company directors. Some of our work has been used by over 9 million people, recognised by the Apple Design Award, taken the front cover of *Wired* magazine, launched companies and hit television, cinema and mobile screens around the world. I speak often with emerging talent, from illustrators to film-makers and students at universities across both the UK and USA. At this point it will be no revelation for me to say that all of these people believe pursuing creativity means having to fight for your work, your career, and to keep everything you do a labour of love.

It's not always rewarding or fun, and sometimes the clock turning to 3am is much more noticeable. But you battle through. Every individual who simply can't imagine *not* making things – the people who want to inspire others, make great things and be respected for them – are the ones who will shape much of the future. And there are plenty of challenges that need solving.

So this book is an exploration of creative potential. Six stories, six chapters, all widely applicable, on how to get the most from our creativity. Stories I intend to let influence me for as long as possible and guide me to produce the best work I can. It is a book I began writing with the hope that sharing them and the ideas they represent would first and foremost help and inspire young creative people in any discipline – students, graduates and young professionals. But it is also humbly presented to anyone, of any age, who can't live without being creative – and the people who can help them realise their ambitions, be they educators, managers, CEOs or otherwise.

Youthful thinking

There are a lot of stories in this book, tales that show why creativity favours intuition, the merits of exploration, creative purpose, the importance of learning and play, and the necessity of daring to fail.

All these are vital examples of the value of *youthful thinking*. This is an idea once framed by Vincent Van Gogh, who remarked: *"It is a pity that, as one gradually gains experience, one loses one's youth."* With Van Gogh, I believe that creativity in whatever discipline is something best practised by embracing useful characteristics of youth. You don't have to be young for that. These characteristics lie within all of us and these stories are simply reminders how to make the most of them. Inherent in this belief is the wholly undeniable but often undervalued merit of every young designer, storyteller, entrepreneur or creative thinker.

This book has contributions and interviews from a handful of people whom I consider to be some of the most inspiring individuals in the world. From Michael Wolff, co-founder of Wolff Olins and widely believed to be the leading authority on brands, to Jamie Oliver – a phenomenon of the food world, TED Prize winner and one of Fast Company's Most Creative People.

Spark for the Fire is intended for those who want to excel like them. It's for the people who are passionate about what they want to do. So passionate it makes them mad enough to think they can impact the world for the better by doing it. It is for anyone wishing to put their imagination to use, professionally or otherwise. Lastly, this book is for the youthful: in age, experience or attitude – and those who want to be – whether to kick-start a career or reignite an established one.

Read this book. Scribble in it, lose your bookmark and bend the pages. Most importantly, continue the conversation with others when you're done, because now more than ever is the perfect time to spark the fire of creativity.

Ian Wharton

WWW.IANWHARTON.COM

@IANWHARTON

#SPARKFORTHEFIRE

I

EMBRACE THE RIDICULOUS

"Every child is an artist. The problem is how to remain an artist once we grow up."

— PABLO PICASSO

At what point in our lives do we best exercise our imagination? The kind of imagination where we allow ourselves to surrender all influence of experience, knowledge and rationality in favour of pure creativity – openly and without restraint. The kind of imagination that is most full of *potential*?

When I was nine-years-old, I played 'Johnny B. Goode' live on stage with a five-piece band called *The Starlighters*. I remember it vividly, stood in front of the microphone, suited, red Gibson guitar in hand. The crowd had never heard anything like it. Scarcely an inch of dance floor went unused. The date was 12 November 1955 – The Enchantment Under the Sea Dance.

I don't care what anyone told me, for a few days after watching *Back to the Future* (1985) the first time, I *was* Marty McFly. It was me on that stage playing Chuck Berry's infamous 12-bar blues. Sure, I might not have really had the band, or the time machine, but as far as my imagination led me to believe I had just rocked a room full of 1950s kids at Hill Valley High School.

Big kids

That iconic scene in *Back to the Future* had a profound impact on my childhood. Fantasy aside, I locked myself in my bedroom and refused to surface until I could play that damn song on the guitar.

What fascinates me is why the nine-year-old version of me was so determined to accomplish that one particular goal. Perhaps the better question is: what was the driving force behind that desire to excel?

I think the answer is a simple one. As a child, I believed that my day-dreams were *completely* attainable in real life. At that point any distinction between reality or otherwise was blurry at best. I never asked them, but I'm certain all my friends at the time believed the same. As, I'm sure, did you.

Something inspiring struck up against my imagination, and from that collision came a newly ignited passion. Learning that song became an outright labour of love. I knew that if I put the effort into my ambition, *anything was possible*. I just lacked the words to explain it at the time.

Nineteen years of growing up later, what has changed? I might watch an episode of *24* and say to myself, "Damn, it would be pretty cool to be Jack Bauer." The difference is I'm not then running around my London apartment fending off make-believe assassins as they burst through my windows.

How boring.

And ultimately, how limiting.

The youthful mind is capable of anything. We know it, and say it frequently, and yet many of us, myself included, are still guilty of involuntarily disengaging parts of it as we get older.

We start paying more attention to process, reason, etiquette. We're bombarded by all the overwhelming and serious things life has to throw at us, and the part of our brain that commands cognitive control and inhibition rolls up its sleeves at the age of 25[1] and starts calling the shots.

Self-control is a necessity in many aspects of life, but creativity can be traded for safety and efficiency as a result. However, the youthful mind never dies entirely; it can always be revived. The useful characteristics of youth are some of the most astonishing and under-valued commodities we have available to us throughout life. Youthful thinking simply means adopting a continual appreciation of their value.

Consider for a moment someone who exemplifies the idea of youthful thinking, one of the best storytellers in the world and Pixar's chief creative officer, John Lasseter. In a *Meet the Film-Maker* event at the Regent Street Apple store in London, Lasseter spoke of his most notable moments at Pixar. Above all, he proudly confessed to being "a big kid".

Lasseter's work and boundless creative energy is proof alone he is in possession of something most people accidentally let go. The ability to always be astonished. To exaggerate and be madly enthusiastic about simple things. To fantasise, be willing to learn, get carried away and embellish things. To immediately and wholeheartedly fall in love with the idea of doing something and that anything,

---

[1]   A study from the Medical Research Council, Cognition and Brain Sciences Unit in Cambridge, England, highlights how prefrontal regions of the brain responsible for self-regulation mature at the age of 25 and that self-regulation depletion (SRD) is confined to younger populations. Dahm T, Neshat-Doost HT, Golden A-M, Horn E, Hagger M, et al. (2011) *Age Shall Not Weary Us: Deleterious Effects of Self-Regulation Depletion Are Specific to Younger Adults.*

absolutely anything, is possible. As a result he is responsible for some of the most iconic stories ever told. He has created the world's first fully computer-animated feature film, revolutionised the animation industry, entertained millions and helped Pixar become the multi-billion-dollar studio that it is today. A studio, furthermore, that is deliberately structured to encourage the kind of playful and explorative nature we have as children, with highly personalised workspaces and a giant atrium that allows casual interactions to be made with people from all departments.

I invite you to look at any inspiring entrepreneur, film-maker, writer, artist, designer – anyone at the top of their field making waves or redefining what was thought possible. I'll wager they openly exercise these characteristics.

Clement Stone (1902–2002), businessman and author of *The Success System That Never Fails,* said: "*Whatever the mind can conceive and believe, it can achieve.*" This is a way of thinking that is fundamentally grounded in youth. Unrestricted imagination is a compelling force and leads to astonishing things. Youthful thinking provides the foundation for unlocking creative potential by giving ourselves and those around us the right conditions to excel.

It can even make a nine-year-old Marty McFly.

Experience and instinct

A problem with a number of industries is that they place a great deal of value on a person's experience alone. It's something of an unwritten law. 'The longer you have been here, the better you are!'

Not long ago I attended a D&AD President's Lecture celebrating the past 50 years of design and advertising. On the panel were three creative legends: Lord Puttnam, Sir Alan Parker and Bob Gill. The insights shared from their accomplishments since the 1960s were staggering. I sat thinking not only what a privilege it was to witness first-hand the value of their combined knowledge, but also how their collective creative calibre was just as impressive when they were in their 20s.

The same can be said of Bill Gates, Steve Jobs, William Hewlett and countless others. The defining and inspired moments that forged their respective companies often came in their youth. The purpose of this book is certainly not to brush aside the validity of experience, but rather to illustrate why, when it comes to creativity, there are better places for the emphasis to lie. Especially when the common metric used to define experience is simply time. There are much more meaningful ways to asses the value of creative potential of people: by the things they have done, successfully or otherwise. Here's a short story to illustrate what I mean.

"Ian, I've been thinking," said one of my earliest clients. *"What can we do creatively with an owl?"*

Ten years ago, at the unencumbered age of 16, I opened a limited company and set out to find my first paid work as a creative. For the record, I had absolutely no idea what I was doing. There were only two things I knew for certain: I needed a way of proving (or selling) my ability to the people I approached, and something unique to offer them. A way to add value. My portfolio had fewer pages than instructions for an electric toothbrush, but the innate youthful confidence we all have at that age was sufficiently daring not to be affected by it. The owl-intrigued client was an award-winning photographer by the name of Victor Trusch. The brief was quite simple: to showcase his remarkable and eccentric collection of work online. And I use the term 'eccentric' with complete admiration.

Looking back, although failing to acknowledge their significance at the time, those eight words from Victor – possibly never before strung together in the history of the English language – led to the second most vital lesson I have learned in my career. And there was only ever one possible response.

"Screw it, let's get an owl and find out."

More specifically we recruited not one owl, but two. There was casting. We set up a crude blue-screen in Victor's studio and hired someone with camera equipment to carry out filming. My insight into the practice of visual effects accompanying this activity was fuelled solely by the fact I had recently watched a *Lord of the Rings* behind-the-scenes DVD.

The goal, then, devoid of any reality as to whether or not I could pull it off, was to film the owl (with its understudy waiting backstage), remove the backdrop in post-production and perch it on the top corner of the website. As the site loaded it would remain completely static, nothing more than an ornament. Only after ten seconds or so would the owl make one subtle movement, then freeze for ten seconds. Then move again, and so on.

The viewer would see something out the corner of their eye and say, *"Did that owl just move?!"* Then stick around for another ten seconds to find out.

Ridiculous.

But also genius. Albeit accidental.

However bizarre, this feature provided an immediate talking point, something that distinguished Victor's site from those of thousands of other photographers. It was an unexpected delight that engrossed people enough to keep them exploring and sharing the experience with others. The site had over 50,000 unique hits in the first month and won a handful of awards, but more importantly got a host of people talking about Victor's brand and introduced it to an entirely new audience.

The achievement of the project markedly surpassed what we had set out to accomplish. Happy client. Famous owl.

The significance of this ten-year-old story is that from all the projects I have done in the time since, it is still the best example I have to illustrate a key component of unlocking potential. *Creativity favours intuition.*

Sat opposite Victor, experience and reason would almost certainly have taught me to diplomatically dodge his request, to file it away as nothing more than a ridiculous flight of imagination. Attaching live owls to the masthead isn't exactly Web Design 101.

But as it turned out, the ridiculous was full of potential. Had I jumped to the rational, self-regulated response, it would have been without any exploration whatsoever. An action that immediately limits the potential for innovation.

As we progress through our careers, we gather all sorts of experience and assign it a compelling value. It's that experience we have come to believe will get us the new job, the pay rise, the perfect project or the client we've always wanted. At the same time, our minds can become more literal, more restrained by what we know for sure. Our field of vision narrows. We close off all kinds of possibilities because we feel as though we should subject our creativity to more conscious reasoning, and be less receptive to the ridiculous (or to the reenactment of our favourite inspiring movie scenes).

And this is *completely* counter-intuitive to creativity.

Rory Sutherland is the vice-chairman of Ogilvy Group UK and former president of the Institute of Practitioners in Advertising. He is also the industry's chief proponent of behavioural sciences and recently the co-founder of #ogilvychange, a company which combines leading behavioural academic research with the communication expertise of the Ogilvy Group.

RORY SUTHERLAND: *You might argue that when you get older you have more things to connect. That can work both ways – you may think that you have so many things to connect that you just start shutting down avenues. When you're young and naive, perhaps you basically make the decision that 'I have X and Y therefore I'll try to make something with X and Y'. Whereas with experience does one actually have so much mental furniture that in order to make the choice bearable, as your mental attic gets fuller and fuller, you fall back more on formula?*

The problem here is that every great new idea, every new challenge, every opportunity can seem ridiculous, illogical, out of place. All too often we are quick to disregard great ideas or new ventures before they gain any momentum, largely because we haven't seen or heard of them before. They are uncharted territory, but instead of being trailblazed they never even get explored. Reason steps in and we start to second-guess. It was the fortunate circumstances of the owl project with Victor – having no real deadline, budget to speak of, or laurels to rest on – that meant I had no restrictions on creativity. Not even my own: the things I didn't know how to do I figured I would solve later. They were a problem for Future Ian. Because of these factors, every decision I made was based on gut feeling. No second-guessing. No self-regulation.

An important principle applied to the best projects, then, is: *release all restrictions and preconceptions and always trust your gut.*

Over a decade later, I am acutely aware I subject new creative projects to conscious debate far more than in earlier years. Youthful thinking is a reminder for me not to overindulge in reasoning or burden the work with convention – to prompt myself to be more willing to embrace something radical. Ridiculous even. It's important to look at projects like an outsider and to experiment, to have the confidence to say stupid or illogical things and to remember that while exercising creativity, at least initially, there are no wrong answers.

Edward de Bono, originator of the notion of lateral thinking, refers to this approach as 'Intermediate Impossibles': thinking that is deliberately contrary to logic and free of restraint that provides a stepping stone to the right solution. It's a question of allowing bizarre connections to flow and *then* using your intuition to decide whether or not any lead to a breakthrough.

RORY: *There are, of course, large parts of business where you don't want excessive experimentation or creativity. When I fly on an aircraft with British Airways I don't want to think the engineers who check the wheel nuts are wildly experimental people going, 'Hey, let's try anti-clockwise this time for a laugh.'*

A dependence on convention is rightly important at times, then – the important thing is to spot when it could be a hindrance. But in the fundamentals of exercising imagination, the precursor to any creative output, you will be better rewarded by thinking young. Relying on reason alone escorts creative thinking wilfully into mediocrity because it is based on precedent rather than innovation.

The trouble is that intuition is happy to purr away quietly in the subconscious. Reasoning, on the other hand, is loud and hard to ignore.

Do now, think later

In a paper called *The Collapse of Sensemaking in Organizations* (1993), Karl E. Weick tells a story of a tribe of Naskapi Indians and their ritual for planning a day's hunt. Stay with me. The Naskapi locate game by holding the shoulder bones of reindeer over a fire until they crack under the heat. The direction in which the bones crack decides which way the tribe sets out in search of food. And Weick observes that the ritual – for all its illogicality – works.

How?

Firstly, stock isn't depleted by knowledge of past hunts. Secondly, it makes sure the Naskapi go out confidently together, with no arguing or second-guessing. They have complete unanimity, even though the base reason for it is daft.

Like these cracks in the smouldering bones, the *randomness of instinct* is sometimes exactly what we need. The idea that instinctive decisions can produce the best results is also something supported by Gerd Gigerenzer from the Max Planck Institute for Human Development. Gigerenzer suggests that instinctive choices can indeed serve us better than decisions which we think to be rational based on calculation or prior experience. You wouldn't want to catch a tennis ball by first trying to calculate its trajectory mathematically, for example.

Instinctive decisions mean we are policing our behaviour less and relying more on what is important to creativity. The un-policed brain is, after all, what it means to be creative. The rationality of a policed brain also brings about a fundamental double standard.

RORY: *Rationality is its own justification. If you're a creative person you'll have to take your ideas to people much more rational than you are. They'll do a feasibility study, investigate return on investment, look at it from six different angles and decide whether or not it works. Creativity is constantly policed by logic, whereas logic is never policed by creativity. You never get a team saying, 'We've done the numbers, it all stacks up, but before I take it to the board I'm going to show it to some really wacky people to see if there's a better way of doing it.'*

Rationality affects businesses where the opposite of instinct – number-crunching – is far easier to defend. In the hierarchy of a manager-run business, rationality is the easiest way to give grounds for a decision. If the decision fails, at least it had an empirical underpinning you can point to. It is measurable and backs are covered. Just at the cost of innovation.

Doing what is measurable is not the same as doing what's meaningful. Rory told me one of his more famous illustrations as to how focusing on the former can potentially diminish creative effectiveness in business. Consider the solution a group of engineers arrived at when tasked with improving a train journey between London and Paris. The engineering decision was to spend several billion pounds replacing all the tracks from London to the coast so as to shorten journey time with faster travel over smoother lines. The question would be, is speed the only way to make a journey better? Or is a focus on speed merely rational and unimaginative? Perhaps employing all of the world's top male and female supermodels and paying them to wander up and down the aisles, handing out free

Château Pétrus for the entire duration of the journey, might be a better solution.

RORY: *There would be money left over, and passengers would call for the trains to be slowed down.*

In the film world, one of the UK's greatest talents is Danny Boyle, director of acclaimed films such as *Trainspotting* (1996), *127 Hours* (2010) and *Slumdog Millionaire* (2008) (which earned him an Academy Award).

"Your first film is always— well, you never quite make a film like that again," he says in an interview with Film 4.[2]

"It's an obvious thing to say, but I think you're so naive, it's wonderful. You really are making it up as you go along, how to do it, how to pull it off... The same is true of the Coen Brothers. Their first film Blood Simple, *geniuses though they are now, they've never made a film as good as that. And I don't think – in a funny kind of way – we've ever made a film as good as* Shallow Grave. *[First films] are always your best one, they are always your most honest. You know so little technically, you're just running on adrenaline, and it's a wonderful thing to run a film on."*

There is something I particularly love about this interview – the way Boyle refers to naivety as being "wonderful". Although often used with negative connotations, naive doesn't have to be a dismissive word. If we choose, it can simply mean *natural* or *unaffected*, conditions that drive creativity from instinct.

---

2   Full interview available at Film 4: **www.film4.com/special-features/interviews/ danny-boyle-on-his-first-three-films**

He also says that a first film is "always your most honest", perhaps because, without any precedent, it is the most true to who you are and what you really want to be doing.

The youthful mind, the mind not dampened by reason but driven purely by instinct, has a tremendous willingness to learn and explore. But it also has a real capacity to get things done. Children don't over-analyse what their imaginations dream up, they just act on it. The fact that through most of the owl project I had no idea what I was doing didn't matter. Just as Danny Boyle making it up as he went along didn't matter. And nor should it ever in the early stages of putting imagination to use.

Screenwriter and novelist Frank Cottrell Boyce, writer of the London 2012 Olympics opening ceremony – also directed by Boyle – remembers the team sharing their initial ideas:

> *"Danny created a room where no one was afraid to speak, no one had to stick to their own specialism, no one was afraid of sounding stupid or talking out of turn. He restored us to the people we were before we made career choices – to when we were just wondering."*[3]

It always pays to say 'why not?' or 'anything's possible' first: to wonder, let go of constraints, dream up anything and embrace the ridiculous. Your idea might become a best-selling boy-wizard franchise or a manned mission into space.

Worry about whether it's possible later.

Back shortly. – *Jack Bauer*

---

3   Full interview in *The Guardian*. 'London 2012: opening ceremony saw all our mad dreams come true'. **www.guardian.co.uk/commentisfree/2012/jul/29/frank-cottrell-boyce-olympics-opening-ceremony**

2

CREATIVITY IS TRANSFERABLE

"Twenty years from now you will be more disappointed by the things you didn't do than by the ones you did do. So throw off the bowlines. Sail away from the safe harbour. Catch the trade winds in your sails. Explore. Dream. Discover."

— MARK TWAIN

From early on in education we are taught that in order to become successful we should find a specialisation in our preferred field and stick to it.

"Do one thing, and do it well!"

Not only is this way of thinking continued throughout professional life, it is routinely amplified. Consequently there are millions of people missing out on things they are truly passionate about.

This advice doesn't even have much historical precedent. Consider some 500 years ago telling Leonardo da Vinci, widely regarded as one of the greatest painters and the most diversely talented individuals ever to have lived, to focus solely on painting. Forget the science, the inventing, the writing. Just paint. 'Specialise'. Such advice, had he listened, would have robbed us of much of his epic creativity.

I wonder if it would even have left him a very inspired painter.

The New Renaissance

To suggest that we are only capable of doing one thing to an exceptional standard dramatically undersells human potential. After all, the Renaissance as an era of invention and creativity didn't differ all too greatly from the present day. If you are truly passionate about making something from nothing, and you can make that *thing* a labour of love, you have something that can be applied absolutely anywhere. And today the tools exist freely (or cheaply) enough to act on it straightaway.

Whatever discipline, medium or execution – creativity is 100% transferable.

There is a term used to describe Leonardo da Vinci. It's not often attributed to people anymore, but it is worthy of aspiring to nevertheless: that word is 'polymath.' A polymath is a person of wide-ranging knowledge or learning, someone who has an *insatiable curiosity to excel in every challenge.*

There are many people who are good at what they do. But there are far fewer who also *love* what they do, at least for enough of the time. This is a big problem, not just because it is better if people *do* enjoy what they are doing every day, but also because we have to find the challenges we are passionate about in order to really excel – to be better than good.

Our true abilities can be hidden well out of sight; unless we are particularly fortunate, they may remain that way. So how do we unearth them?

The answer has to involve moving past only practising what we know. In other words, having the freedom and confidence to explore, dream and discover is incredibly important throughout our careers.

Creative people are blessed with the gift of agility. It also means that young creatives, in particular, should feel no rush to consign themselves to a single practice. The consequences of specialising too early will ultimately only hamper potential. When we are continually hired to do what we first become good at – the common way talent is utilised, especially in big organisations – desire to learn can quickly decrease and vast potential can go unused.

The safety of routine and a steady salary may even stop someone looking for new ways to challenge themselves altogether. And what could be worse? It conflicts with our natural drive to fully understand what we are capable of, and at the very least heightens a susceptibility to burnout.

Even on a neurological level it cannot be the way we are meant to function. A mind denied challenges, repeating the same thing over and over, switches to autopilot. The brain relies on the same old processes, and like any other activity we perform habitually and without inspired focus, it learns to perform them half-asleep to conserve energy. But the last thing you want is your creative work to take on all the dynamism and innovation of your morning dress routine or commute to work.

Naturally, organisations as much as individuals ought to be concerned by this. Solving a new problem – problems that didn't exist a year ago – is a huge part of being a successful creative business today. And it's much harder to do that with employees who are denied (deliberately or accidentally) the space to be as creative and multidisciplinary as possible, or who are hired for specialist experience rather than creative breadth. Life isn't straightforward. Career ladders probably ought not to be either.

A multi-creative life

The career of the next person we'll hear from is a living witness to the transferable nature of creativity. David Puttnam, Lord Puttnam of Queensgate, spent 30 years as an independent producer of award-winning films, including notable titles such as *The Mission* (1986), *Bugsy Malone* (1976), *Midnight Express* (1978) and *Chariots of Fire* (1981), which earned him an Academy Award. He has served as the vice-president and chair of trustees at the British Academy of Film & Television Arts (BAFTA) and was awarded a BAFTA Fellowship in 2006, the same year that saw him become Commander of the Order of Arts and Letters in France.

Having retired from film in 1998 to focus on education and the environment, he has since founded the National Teaching Awards, served as chair of the General Teaching Council, president of UNICEF UK and a trustee of the Eden Project, the Tate Gallery and the Science Museum. David is currently chancellor of the Open University, chairman of advertising agency Profero and founding chair of the National Endowment for Science, Technology and the Arts (NESTA).

LORD PUTTNAM: *Having been brought up in the London of the 1950s, I became an utterly unapologetic product of the 60s – part of a generation who were reminded by the US civil rights leader, Eldridge Cleaver, that, "If you're not prepared to be part of the answer, then you're almost certainly part of the problem!" Legislators were gently warned not to "stand in the doorway or block up the hall" and to "get out of the way now if you can't lend a hand". And in fairness, the times they really were 'a-changing'.*

At 17 I landed my first job. It was in publishing, which even then struck me as being an incredibly dusty and complacent affair, one that seemed to almost glory in its Dickensian fustiness. In effect it was an entire world that had to die before it could be reinvented. After a very short while I fled into advertising, an industry that became in just about every respect my university. After a couple of false starts I found myself working with people who saw change far more as an opportunity than a threat.

My next stop was the film industry which, in the late 60s, was still defending working practices that were firmly set in the early 1950s. It was entirely unprepared for, and ultimately devastated by, the changes forced upon it in the mid-80s. Rank and EMI, the incumbent cinema chains, were to all intents and purposes a licensed duopoly, and as such were far more engaged in avoiding change than embracing it. I found myself staggered at how complacent and un-self-critical were the industry's day-to-day working practices. Its inability to recognise that values, especially of the young, were fundamentally changing was a very serious structural weakness.

Those of us arriving in the House of Lords in 1997 (especially those from the private sector) believing there was a serious role to play, were genuinely stunned at the lack of resources available to allow us to fulfil our (possibly inflated) expectations. We encountered almost total confusion as to whether it was a place of work, or a kind of extended 'club' with additional, if important, legislative responsibilities.

Having along the way served on the boards of a variety of public institutions, from the Tate Gallery, through the Royal Academy to the Science Museum, I came to believe that only through a continuous re-appraisal of purpose, and the degree to which they could be seen to be addressing the legitimate and changing expectations of the public, could institutions ensure they remained relevant to the society they were created to serve.

I appreciate there is something of an experiential pattern emerging here. Early on I'd found publishing to be arranged principally for the comfort of publishers, not their readers. The advertising world I joined in the late 50s was in many cases blissfully unaware and unprepared for the social upheaval of the 60s. The film industry of the early 70s was organised far more for the benefit of those running it than their audience. It was the emergence of a younger generation of filmmakers and executives who ensured that change became possible and who rescued the industry from what looked like terminal decline.

An American Jesuit priest, Anthony de Mello, writes very well on the subject of our innate lack of ability to question our motives in either resisting or promoting change. It is young people who are best positioned to understand the importance of change and to refuse the status quo.

In the case of every one of the sectors and institutions I've worked in, the argument against change has always been built around what I call 'exceptionalism'. This is the belief that, whilst change elsewhere may be desirable and even necessary, we are a special case – immune to painful improvement!

The massive challenge for the creative industries as a whole is now to meet the changing expectations of a generation of young people who expect, as a matter of course, to participate in making and shaping their world, and not to simply be passive recipients of whatever is handed down. In my experience, any creative sector that does not respond to that challenge is destined to wither on the vine. But I believe that the enormous wealth and diversity of youthful talent in our creative industries is more than capable of rising to that challenge and seizing the huge opportunities of the digital age.

Screw the comfort zone

In recent years there has been a lot of talk about the '10,000 hour rule'. This is the idea that the key to success in any field is a matter of practising a single specific task for a total of 10,000 hours. It is an attractive theory and well-written cases have been made for it.

But I'm not sure it's entirely true.

Now, working hard, harder than your competitors, will *of course* create an undeniable advantage if done intelligently. However, the 10,000 hour rule can be a dangerous concept for creative potential if misinterpreted, even if we forgive the immediate issues of who has the right to define 'success' or 'mastery' for any other individual – and that the fairly arbitrary number of 10,000 from the original K. Anders Ericsson study could even discourage people from making a move to explore a passion. Quantity is hardly a sufficient unit to define how something such as imagination can be put to use.

And sticking to one practice doesn't guarantee mastery, nor is it definitive. It has the potential to make someone an accomplished painter, but it won't make them a Leonardo. It could even prevent the discovery of something they love.

In other words, there is a world of difference between 10,000 hours of passion and 10,000 hours of tolerance.

Ideas, stories, the creative sparks required to solve a problem are unforeseeable and ineffable. In the same way good ideas rarely materialise during forced group brainstorms, we can't arrive at the point where we are most creative by mindless repetition. Great ideas and opportunities arise by chance, when we least expect them. The best way of finding them is with a willingness to adapt and catapult ourselves into new things.

I love the phrase *"continuous re-appraisal of purpose"* from Lord Puttnam. That's how we learn. That's how businesses progress. And perhaps most significantly, that's how we discover something that inspires us most – the starting point for outperformance.

Equally, unless we pay particularly close attention, doing the same thing over and over doesn't necessarily mean we get any better at it. In his book *Moonwalking with Einstein* (2011), Joshua Foer, a journalist and US memory champion, calls it the 'OK Plateau'. This is the place we get to where we stop getting appreciably better at something.

> *"When people first learn to use a keyboard, they improve very quickly from sloppy single-finger pecking to careful two-handed typing, until eventually the fingers move so effortlessly across the keys that the whole process becomes unconscious and the fingers seem to take on a mind of their own. At this point, most people's typing skills stop progressing. They reach a plateau. If you think about it, it's a strange phenomenon. After all, we've always been told that practice makes perfect, and many people sit behind a keyboard for at least several hours a day in essence practicing their typing. Why don't they just keep getting better and better?"*

Foer goes on to show that in order to get better, the task has to be brought back under conscious control. You have to push yourself past where you are comfortable, notice the failures you make, and learn from them.

Setting ourselves challenges and stepping out from comfort zones is how we improve and give ourselves the opportunity to excel rather than stagnate. Being successful at one craft could simply mean a person has identified a process that works and can repeat it. Not the worst thing to be guilty of, but it does reduce the possibility for new discoveries. And if there's one thing that should never be standardised, it's creativity.

Telling stories

A phrase I use throughout this book is 'labour of love'. Projects that are a labour of love, by their nature, distinguish themselves from the mediocre. They are the projects that define a career or a company and are the ones we are always happy to tell the story of to our peers. They make an impact and guide us to discover something great, perhaps even life-changing.

What is my greatest labour of love?

It's the project that I am still most proud to have been involved with and the one that has so far made the biggest contribution to my career.

Until mid-2007, a bachelor of arts course ran at Cumbria Institute of the Arts that taught the broad practices and principles of animation, advertising, 3D, film and interactivity. Uniquely, there was no specialisation prescribed by the lecturers. Students worked independently and in teams across disciplines, and open-mindedness towards every corner of the creative industries was encouraged. The extremely rare nature of this syllabus also provided a free reign for each student to assign their graduation project to whatever would excite and inspire them the most.

This was Mark Twain's advice in action.

Given the influence this project would have on my degree, the logical part of my brain told me to focus my energy on something I found comfortable, something that made use of the experience I had accumulated from digital projects before university – a website or digital campaign.

But more than anything else at the time, myself and classmate Ed Shires were entirely in love with the work of Pixar. I loved the stories they told; how beautiful and inventive they were, the way they engaged an undivided spectrum of human emotion and how they appealed to children and adults in equal measure.

How did they achieve this time and again? What was at the core of these stories?

These became the questions we pored over. All we knew was that it was something we had to explore. Even if we could only replicate the results to a fractional degree, it was worth pursuing. So our degree project became a short animated film called *Solar* (2007).

Against all reason we followed only instinct and began writing the film. During two months of pre-production as the story took shape, we found our focus: the process of night and day, the relationship between the sun and the moon. We reimagined that process as if it involved Brunel-esque mechanics, with the sun and the moon relying on two characters for their successful operation. In turn, the life of these two characters relied on night and day.

It was this idea of an infinite and harmonious loop that seemed a good scenario into which we could inject an inciting incident. It was also the idea that, following our pitch, prompted our otherwise supportive lecturers to unanimously tell us: "It's too ambitious, it can't be done in the time you have," and, "It's too complicated a story to tell."

These were words Ed and I were not expecting to hear. But perhaps we never really did hear them. We spent the next seven months in production.

The things we want to do

In 2005 the best innovator of his era, Steve Jobs, gave a now-famous commencement address to the graduating class of Stanford University. It included three stories about the most pivotal points in his life, stories that reflected on the importance of pursuing your dreams. One particular thing he said stuck with me:

> *"For the past 33 years, I have looked in the mirror every morning and asked myself: 'If today were the last day of my life, would I want to do what I am about to do?' Whenever the answer has been 'No' for too many days in a row, I know I needed to change something."*

The quote raises an interesting question: *what are the properties of the things we want to do?* I don't think many of us ask ourselves that question, or would necessarily know how to answer it. Is it something that inspires us? That excites us? That will make an impact? That will challenge us and help us develop? Something that is a labour of love? I believe there to be one word which sums up the things we truly want to do: *passion*. As a constant advocate of creativity, especially in education, I'm a great admirer of Sir Ken Robinson. In his book *The Element* (2009) he talks wonderfully on how to find our passion:

> *"The Element is the meeting point between natural aptitude and personal passion. [People in their element] find that time passes differently and that they are more alive, more centred, and more vibrant than at any other times. Being in their element takes them beyond the ordinary experiences of enjoyment or happiness. They connect with something fundamental to their sense of identity,*

purpose, and well-being. Being there provides a sense of self-revelation,
of defining who they really are and what they're really meant to be
doing with their lives."

Having worked with Jamie Oliver and his organisation for a little over four years, I consider him to be a perfect example of someone in his element – simultaneously committed to what he loves and open to new ideas. Jamie is without question one of the most inspiring people I have met and possesses the most astonishing work ethic – one reason why he is so successful. I feel a more important reason for his success is that I have yet to encounter anyone who is more passionate about what they do than he is. It is genuine and remarkable.

It's how he has managed to bring joy to so many people around the world and champion positive change in health through better education in food. His passion for doing what he does is infectious and his success is a by-product of that. Sir Ken would unquestionably say he is in his Element.

What is fascinating about Jamie is that he was lucky enough to discover his passion at a relatively early age. He began working as a chef at one of the country's best restaurants, the River Café, the very place he was discovered, in his early 20s. It would be easy to end the story shortly after that.

When you consider everything that Jamie has achieved since then as a television personality, an educator, entrepreneur and writer of 18 cookbooks – including one of the fastest-selling non-fiction books in history – there is something else contributing to his accomplishments.

While sat overlooking an illuminated St Paul's Cathedral in one of his adjacent restaurants, Jamie told me the story of the serendipitous circumstances that launched him to TV fame. Those circumstances came from dedication to his job and team. His phenomenal success extending beyond that key moment is down to his willingness to explore, to learn, and see what else he is capable of. In other words, he has succeeded by *not* practising only what he knows for sure.

Cooking was the catalyst, in the same way computer programming was for Mark Zuckerberg. What they have in common is their openness to challenges and uncertainty. That's why things got interesting. It's also why I had the good fortune to work with Jamie while I was the creative partner of app design and development company Zolmo: he was one of the first global brands to experiment with mobile.

The executive creative director at one of the UK's most-awarded advertising agency AMV BBDO and former D&AD president, Paul Brazier, has a similar story ...

PAUL BRAZIER: *It was obvious early on in my life that my skills didn't lie in the academic world. And I think that's true of a lot of creative people. But just because I didn't shine academically it didn't mean I lacked intelligence – it just meant I thought differently.*

I tried a career as a footballer first, until I was cruelly thwarted by a lack of talent. Then I discovered art. I was obsessed. In the holidays I explored every creative opportunity I could: trying to be an illustrator, enquiring about set design, product design, experimenting with photography and typography.

Thankfully someone suggested I might be interested in advertising. I managed to get an interview at Cogent Elliot, probably the best agency in London at the time. They liked my portfolio and offered me a placement. Soon enough, it turned into a proper job. I then spent four years at WCRS, and for the last 20 years I have been at AMV BBDO.

The difficulty a lot of creatives have is that they tend to be interested in the whole world of creativity. They can turn their hands to a lot of things. This is a fantastic asset but it's also a hindrance. It makes it difficult to know which career to pursue. But one thing I learned relatively late in my career is that you don't have to choose what you do straightaway. After all, how many app designers knew that's what they wanted to do ten years ago? Apps weren't invented then.

The moral is, we should take our time and keep an open mind.

Following your imagination

I mentioned earlier that *Solar* is the project I am still most proud to have worked on, the one that has propelled my career the furthest. The reason for this is quite simple: it is the project that inspired the most passion.

Every single day during the seven months of production I couldn't wait to see what progress would be made. There was never a moment where I didn't appreciate what we were doing or what we were trying to accomplish. And in that frame of mind, *"It can't be done"* is never heard.

It is also the project that led me to discover something I loved: animated film. This was a discovery made purely by stepping out from a comfort zone and into the unknown. The best projects, the ones where every day we wake up and say *"This is what I want to be doing"* will be the ones that make the biggest impact on ourselves, our companies, industries and beyond. Even if they go against rational thought, or what others consider to be best.

If for too long the thought of your activities in the day ahead don't inspire you, excite you, or instil passion – *change what you are doing.* Waste zero time making things you don't want to be known for. Look outside your immediate interests and make connections beyond the finite world of specialisation. And never think there's a field or profession you can't be in, or a challenge you can't rise to.

Some may say, *"Do one thing, and do it well!"* I would prefer: Do whatever your imagination and desire demands of you.

And then you can't help but do it well.

3

BEWARE INVISIBILITY

"Your vision of where or who you want to be is the greatest asset you have." – PAUL ARDEN

The quote opening this chapter comes from the legendary book *It's Not How Good You Are, It's How Good You Want To Be* (2003). As an executive creative director at Saatchi & Saatchi whose tenure extended almost two decades, the author, Paul Arden (1940–2008) was responsible for some of Britain's most memorable and successful advertising campaigns. The topic covered in this chapter and articulated by this famous quote is one of the most valuable in the whole book.

You are only as good as your ability to sell yourself.

For the purpose of this book, 'sell' has two meanings:

I. TO MAKE KNOWN THE THINGS WE
HAVE ALREADY ACHIEVED

i.e. Showcasing our talents and ability in the work and things we have done.

2. TO COMMUNICATE THE THINGS WE
HAVE YET TO ACHIEVE

i.e. Expressing our goals and vision of where or who we want to be.

When combined, these two halves of self-promotion create a fulfilling career carried with momentum. Over the next few pages I want to show you that neglecting the process of 'selling', or even using one half of self-promotion without the other, can be restricting. Getting this right in itself is an art form that should accompany or be embedded in the very way you work.

This idea isn't about *introversion vs. extroversion* or how the traits of one personality type are inherently more likely to result in success. Many creatives and entrepreneurs are shy people. For some that is arguably the root of their genius and introversion is signalled as a quality.

While I do believe in the merits of 'selling', I don't mean to suggest you must be outwardly flamboyant or loud. The reality is that someone can still be exceptionally successful without being either. In fact, you could argue the internet suddenly unleashed a huge amount of creative ability from people who are shy. What this chapter explores is that it's perfectly OK to create opportunities for ourselves, that selling can lead to great things and can be done without negative side-effects.

A little context

Throughout my career I have met and worked with people of glorious creative ability, many of whom, students and professionals alike, hate the thought of self-promotion. Even with the means that technology and the internet provide us, it strikes me that too many people are reluctant to sell the story of their ability, their goals, and the work they have done.

It's not something that is necessarily more common in students; it can be carried throughout a career. And although I am frequently told *"I'm not good at promoting myself"* or *"I hate doing any self-promotion"*, I don't often hear a convincing rationale. An understandable fear lies at the bottom of it: *"If I tell people how good I am or how good I want to be, they'll think I'm arrogant!"*

In truth, as long as the 'selling' is grounded in basic humility – and with the right context or positioning – that particular stigma is entirely mythical. The reality is this. If you are in the film industry, you are in the industry of selling. If you are making apps, advertising or content of any kind, you are in the industry of selling. Artists have to sell themselves. Writers also. If you are a designer, lawyer, musician, accountant or teacher, you have to sell either your vision, expertise or end product. Or all three.

Tim Lindsay is the chief executive of D&AD, a charity now in its 50th year, with the aim of informing, educating and inspiring creative excellence around the world. The D&AD Pencils are widely deemed the ultimate recognition of creativity and leave an impressive legacy – an archive of five decades of the most innovative creative work in design and advertising.

D&AD also plays a role in stimulating creative education by putting profits back into programmes for students and teachers. Before joining the organisation, Tim worked at some of the top advertising agencies, including account executive roles at Lowe Howard-Spink, serving as the joint managing director of Bartle Bogle Hegarty (BBH), chairman of Publicis UK and president of TBWA for UK and Ireland.

TIM LINDSAY: *Back in 1962 there was a group of photographers, graphic designers and advertising people who realised there was no way of them getting credit for their work. There was no way of them saying 'I'm proud of that, and I did it.' That's really why D&AD started. It is about acknowledging the most creative work in the world.*

Most companies talk about the importance of creativity and innovation. Some of them mean it, some of them mean it and do something about it, but most don't really mean it and don't do anything about it. That's why a lot of communication design in the broad sense is mediocre.

People still don't understand the importance of it, and there are so many pressures on them that it doesn't get done in the right way. It's a distressing waste of money and talent, but most of all it's just ineffective – the good stuff still works better than the bad stuff.

We don't set out to prove this, but what we're about is increasing efficiency of business communication and design, increasing the effectiveness of those programmes by trying to create a better environment in terms of the relationship between people who commission the work and the people who do it, and trying to create a better environment within agencies themselves – which are often quite exploitative, particularly in the way they recruit new talent. All of these things need someone like us to focus on, to be a voice for doing things better.

At the beginning of Lowe Howard-Spink, there was an itinerant art director called Tony Kaye. He was completely wild and unpredictable and always worked on his own. One day Tony asked my mate and partner at the agency, Jerry Judge, for career advice on how to present himself. Jerry said to him: "Honest Craftsman".

And he went away and reinvented himself as this. He became one of the most-awarded directors in D&AD history and went on to

Hollywood, directing American History X *(1998). It was a brilliant thing for Jerry to have said.*

The important thing is that people *need a positioning. Brands need a positioning, but people also need a positioning. The briefer the description, the better. And it can be figured out. It's mainly what's true about you.*

The lens that Judge gave to Kaye of *honest craftsman* proved a valuable tool. It was authentic and meaningful, and helped rocket a career by placing it in the right context. At Zolmo we partnered with one of the most authentic global sports figures, Georges St-Pierre. Georges, also known as 'GSP', is a Canadian mixed martial artist and MMA welterweight champion, generally recognised as one of the world's best pound-for-pound fighters and all-round athletes. Behind the success rests ambition and showmanship balanced perfectly with honesty and humility.

When Georges asked his three-million-strong online fan base to set him fitness challenges, he made the decision to film and share each attempt. If a challenge exceeded his ability – for example, an unearthly one-arm pull-up – he didn't hide it. Instead he posted the video of him trying and said:

> *"Well, I can't do this. But I would like to know how can I train myself to be able to do it, so give me some tips! It takes incredible strength, hopefully I can practise it and with your help one day I'll be able to do it."*

Not often does a high-profile champion athlete admit weaknesses, but that's how Georges has garnered so much respect in his field and helped himself to build the tools needed to be a champion. Georges radiates ambition and he demonstrates his ability each time he competes – but he matches it with a desire to learn, to improve and go after things he can't do. Even superhuman brands need work.

As far as communicating the right positioning, Georges' example provides the perfect framework for everything that follows in this chapter. Change the context of *'Set me your fitness challenges'* by removing the humility, and the outcome would have been very different.

The things we have achieved

Carry your mind back to the moment in your childhood when you first learned to ride a bike. Or perhaps when you found the coordination to master a cartwheel, or memorised all the words to your favourite song.

Did you take pleasure in acting out this new talent in private? Or did you rally the attention of every nearby schoolfriend and family-member while you performed it?

You can bet the minute I learned to play 'Johnny B. Goode' from start to finish I dragged my guitar into school and played it for whoever would listen. I'm probably still the only pupil who turned up with a Fender Stratocaster on Bring a Toy Day.

And yes, even I cringe at the thought of that now. But why do I cringe? Why should that be embarrassing to me only now, after all these years?

All children openly seek attention by proudly showcasing the new things they have learned. They don't do this as just an act of self-indulgence; it is coupled with a genuine desire for feedback, to have personal progression acknowledged.

And any parent will tell you that children are in no way sensitive to the opinions of their peers. The response they get is what helps develop them as individuals.

Sensitivity to showcasing these things is built up only with age or in some cases the conclusion of a less-than-encouraging education. Constant self-editing, and minimal sharing, is a direct result. There are a lot of creative freedoms that are surrendered as we grow up, but I'm inclined to believe this one bears the most weight. If we can move beyond the hesitation to open ourselves up to feedback and criticism from people we respect (that's the important bit), the act of self-promotion brings with it some amazing benefits.

One is an openness to taking risks. This is achieved by building up a gradual resistance against the urge to self-edit. Huge discoveries can be had by not regulating possibilities that way. (More on that in Chapter 6.)

Secondly, self-promotion brings recognition, an essential component of developing any career with momentum. I have yet to meet anyone who doesn't want or enjoy their efforts being validated and appreciated by others. Recognition makes the endless hours more fulfilling, stimulates the next stage of a career and will forever inspire and drive you to excel because you are, from that moment on, part of a family of excellence.

But it's not magic. It's the equivalent of a guitar and amp on Bring a Toy Day. To get the D&AD Pencil, or equivalent milestone, you have to sell yourself and the work you have done, to put yourself under the right spotlight. It's not about setting out to write a novel in order to win a Man Booker Prize, or a film to win a BAFTA.

It's about doing something you love that might result in the award. But don't be hesitant to look in that direction once you're done. Recognition and exposure comes only to the people who make themselves visible. We should perhaps all take comfort in knowing that even the Oscars have a submission process.

Lastly, and maybe most importantly, self-promotion also brings collaboration. Collaborations are born out of experiencing a complementary talent of another individual or company – the very way great partnerships are formed.

TIM: *No single individual and no single organisation has all the skills to get everything done. Partnerships between companies and partnerships between individuals within them must be the way forward. And in my observation in 35 years of the business, that propensity to collaborate hasn't been a big feature in a lot of creative people.*

In 1941 a pair of stand-up comedians were separately booked to perform in a show, appropriately titled *Youth Takes a Bow*, at the Nottingham Empire Theatre. Five years later, after another chance encounter, they teamed up once more. They then remained a double act until 1984 – an incredible 43 years later. That is the story of how Morecambe and Wise came to be one of the best-loved British comedy duos.

It would be easy to look at that story and say the partnership was all down to luck or being in the right place at the right time. And we would be absolutely right in thinking that. But serendipity favours people who create the foundations for it.

Ajaz Ahmed has been a big facilitator of milestones in my career. We met during an award ceremony for *Solar*. Ed and I certainly weren't expecting to win, but nor did we ever debate entering. Had we not put ourselves in line for the spotlight, my path may never have crossed Ajaz's. I'll never forget how Ajaz introduced himself either: "I'm from a company called AKQA." Not the CEO opener speech, but humility.

With the abundant sharing opportunities provided by technology – even something as simple as putting a video on YouTube – we would be mad not to take advantage of them to showcase things we have achieved. Even if it means tolerating a Justin Bieber or two.

The things we want to achieve

Ambition, the desire to achieve something beyond what we are currently capable of, has incalculable value if we want to tap our potential. Even so, unaccompanied vision isn't entirely useful. It is vital the goals we set ourselves are selectively aired to the people around us. This is the second part of self-promotion and there are three reasons why we should pay attention to it.

I .

Saying goals out loud solidifies them and provides ground for the first step towards taking action. There is a world of difference between internalising an idea ad infinitum and vocalising it.

Eternally mulling over a goal is a disguised form of procrastination. Say a goal out loud, even to one person, and suddenly it becomes tangible – and tangible things have a presence that can be investigated accordingly. The more public you make your goal, the less willing you will be to change it. This is what bestows your subconscious with the fuel it needs to identify a path to accomplishing it.

Articulating your goals and having the right people take interest will also motivate you to pursue them. The more passionate your 'sell' of what it is you want to accomplish, the more others will become inspired and, in turn, drive you mad until you pull it off. It's easy to underestimate how incentivising a comment as simple as *"I can't wait to see this new project of yours"* or *"Why isn't your book out yet?"* can be.

2 .

If our colleagues, peers, or friends and family aren't aware of our aspirations, they will never be able to help us achieve them. If you want to set up a new company, maybe you already know an investor or your ideal first client.

Anyone who has ever succeeded did so with the help of someone else. Achieving brilliant things is collaborative and always will be.

3 .

Sharing your goals also means standing up for yourself, your company, your colleagues and your work. It is the authentic voice that means things get done in the best way, and that it's fine to say 'no' in order to protect your approach.

TIM: *If you go back to the great agencies of the last 30 or 40 years –
CDP, Saatchi & Saatchi, BBH, and Wieden + Kennedy more recently
– those agencies have stood up for creative people and creative work
by insisting on a standard. And if clients fuck about, they get fired.
CDP fired the Ford motor company and Nestlé. Lowe Howard-Spink
fired Fiat, right in its early days when the account was probably half*

the agency's revenue. If the company has principles, creative people will
want to work there – because they know they'll be stuck up for.

There's also the echoing abyss that separates collaborations and committees. One works, one doesn't and never will. Working with other talented and engaged people to produce the best outcome is always necessary. Feature films are brought together by writers, producers, cast, sound designers, editors, visual effects artists, make-up artists, caterers and countless others. But the vision needs to be driven by one person and one person alone: the director.

It's the director's responsibility to sell that vision, to get each of the stakeholders believing in it, in order to advance it further. It's the same reason sports teams have coaches. Good leaders give room to empower the people they work with, but allowing creativity to become subject to committee is inherently limiting and often the result of something being sold inadequately. Not everyone knows what's best, otherwise they wouldn't have hired you to solve their problem.

TIM: *And clients have planted themselves right in the middle of this process. Because they aren't usually confident in choosing the best work, they've turned it into a multiple-choice scenario. I ran the Levi's business for nine years at BBH. We made 13 commercials in that time, including the launch of 501s. We presented 14 scripts to the client, and the one they didn't make was only because they couldn't afford it. At Lowe's, a group of us ran the Stella Artois account through the 90s. We made eight commercials and we presented eight scripts. There was one the client didn't want because he didn't like the ending. We said in the meeting, "'If you want a different script, you'll have to go with a different agency.'" Why would you dissipate your energy doing three instead of one that was fantastic and pushed as far as you could?*

When it comes to any service industry there are plenty of behavioural biases which can influence people's choice-making, even if they aren't aware of them. In my early 20s I led a brand redesign for a large global organisation. Just as I handed the signed-off site over to the web development team, management forwarded the complete designs to staff who had been at the company ten years or more and asked them to "send any changes to Ian". Not more than an hour later I received a one-line email:

"Make the search box border darker. Thx"

Nothing more. It turned out this person had been with the company since it was founded and up until now hadn't been involved in the redesign at all. He was probably acutely aware of that. Having spent a year battling with an already bloated group of stakeholders, I waited 20 minutes, renamed the file without alterations from 'search_01.jpg' to 'search_02.jpg' and sent it back. Moments later I received a response.

"Much better."

It was a stupid thing to do in hindsight, and one I won't repeat, but all that person wanted was ownership. His aim was to assert authority on the brand based on 20 years service to it, rather than contribute something based on usability or creative insight.

Had he been involved earlier (which he was entitled to be) the relationship could have been managed much better. When the email went out with the phrase "*send changes to ...* " the method of working became irreparably broken.

As the famous David Ogilvy saying goes: "*Search all the parks in all your cities; you'll find no statues of committees.*" So make sure you're doing the selling to the right people from the start. When you have that, sell your vision – whatever it takes – to get people on board. And do it with conviction. Don't give them 15 versions to choose from.

TIM: *But there's a limit to which you can be an insistent individual in an agency. You have to look for partners, people you can team up with and that you intuitively trust. You have to stand up for yourself, you need a boss that stands up for you and an organisation that is doing the right thing.*

And we should know not to settle for anything less. Selling the *things we have achieved* and *things we want to achieve* makes a big impact. Even a life-changing impact.

For further inspiration there is one person in particular we can turn to. He demonstrates perfectly the benefit of selling ambition and ability the right way. Arnold Schwarzenegger.

No, really.

I'll be back

Last Action Hero (1993) is the cult hit film-within-a-film that sees Schwarzenegger playing fictional LA police detective Jack Slater. Uniquely, Arnie also plays himself, as the actor portraying Jack Slater, who even within the film is a fictional star of action films.

I spent 20 minutes trying to write that paragraph. It doesn't even include the scene where Arnie briefly takes on the role of a cigar-smoking Hamlet.

Alongside Schwarzenegger's Jack Slater is Danny Madigan, the boy who finds himself in the parallel world inhabited by Slater and who attempts to convince him of his true identity. At one point he turns to Slater after a trademark one-liner and says, *"You think you're funny, don't you?"* To which Slater responds, *"I know I am. I'm the famous comedian … Arnold Braunschweiger!"*

Though maybe few will be aware, that line is a subtle two-fingers to an earlier day in Schwarzenegger's career; I'll explain why shortly.

Through all of his accomplishments, including those that carried him to become an action star portraying himself playing a fictional action star, Schwarzenegger has never taken himself too seriously. When you look at how altogether brilliant his life-story has been so far, this is an impressive triumph.

How do you go about building three wildly different careers, away from your home country and in a foreign language, and become the epitome of success in all of them? Whether you happen to be a fan like me or not, Schwarzenegger has accomplished a lot – and his successes are a masterclass in the art of selling. The Austrian is a seven-time winner of the Mr. Olympia contest,[4] one of the most recognisable and highly-valued stars in Hollywood, and a politician who has become a champion for climate change as well as a twice-elected Governor of California – the American state with the largest economy.

---

4   Mr. Olympia is the annual international bodybuilding competition held by the International Federation of BodyBuilding & Fitness (IFBB).

How much vision did it take to drive those careers? How much ambition? When asked about his motivation during the filming of *Pumping Iron* (1977), the feature documentary that launched him to fame, he answered: "I always felt like my place was in America, and when I was ten years old I only dreamed of coming to America and being the greatest. I was always impressed by people who could be remembered for hundreds of years, even thousands of years." (Accent optional).

This was a pretty powerful thing to say. Knock it as some might, it is this kind of attitude that fires the heart to accomplish anything. American writer and mythologist Joseph Campbell called it "following your bliss" – going after the things that make you who you are. In doing so "the universe will open doors where there were only walls".

Schwarzenegger wanted to move to America and be "the greatest". He recognised bodybuilding could be his vessel to do so and along the way he became a sports icon who helped create the gym culture we have today. He didn't just lift weights, he lifted an entire industry. His desire evolved into becoming a movie star, and he became one of the most successful and iconic actors in history. In fact, according to Edward Jay Epstein's *The Hollywood Economist* (2010), his appearance in *Terminator 3* (2003) landed him something in the region of $30,000,000 upfront, not including what he brokered from TV and DVD rights: deals almost unheard of in Hollywood at the time.

And from Terminator to Governator, he even said he might have considered running for president if the constitution had been amended to allow foreign citizens to stand. Arnold Schwarzenegger will undoubtedly be remembered for hundreds of years, and he's not even finished.

The question we have to ask ourselves is: where do we want to be? Mr. Olympia? A feature-film star? Governor of California? Or all three?

Whatever your goal, let it be known where you want to be and take pride in saying so. As we get older we tend to concern ourselves too much with the judgement of our peers. It's far too easy to have courageous goals sniggered at or batted away by the cynical, and then to go from there to having no goals at all.

But cynicism is the opposite of creativity and projected only by those not brave enough to pursue their own goals or assign them any conviction. Here's the good news, it's their problem – we can simply pay it no attention.

Schwarzenegger was told countless times by agents that he would never make it as an actor because of his Austrian accent and a surname that wouldn't fit on movie posters – which is what he pokes fun at in *Last Action Hero*. But he found a way. He was told he couldn't go straight to serving as a governor, but rather should serve in lower offices such as city council and mayor's office first. But he broke the rules and found a way.

They won't realise it, but the inevitable naysayers who criticise or badmouth those with searing ambition are only doing a disservice to themselves by cultivating an incapacity to be inspired and therefore an incapacity to be creative. Life is just too short. Passion and belief in ambition is contagious: it's how great leaders inspire those around them to create brilliant things.

Why wouldn't we want to meet and encourage these kinds of people? More importantly, why wouldn't we want to become one of them?

Voicing ambition in any industry also raises the question of perceived value. Not value in a commercial sense such as a salary or the cost of a product, but the intrinsic value an individual can add to any project, company or client. Since we are mostly responsible for assigning this value ourselves, it is something routinely underestimated. The goal of building our brand and value is not to deceive, but to give ourselves the best opportunities and reach our potential. Let me give you an example.

Last year a talented friend and ex-colleague began looking for senior designer jobs in New York. We had worked together at an agency in Manchester where he held an equivalent senior role, and aside from being a good friend he happened to be one of the best designers in the country. In a brief passing comment I suggested he amend the title on his CV to 'art director', then continue his search accordingly. This was not a huge change, just a slight shift in context.

A few months pass and he's working as an art director at a top New York agency, with better pay and more responsibility than that of a senior designer. Just over a year later he's promoted to associate creative director. Further proof of his value, and it certainly won't stop there. Each of us – young or not-so-young – can add value to any organisation, typically a greater value than we let on. Even the best creative people in the world can inadvertently limit their potential by undervaluing themselves.

Don't ask, don't get

When I first moved to London I was working in a similar art director role for a visual effects company called The Mill, best known for its work on *Gladiator* (2000). I was 23 when I joined and considered the work they produced second-to-none. You could take any still image from any of their commercials over the past 20 years and frame it as a work of art.

During my time there the role of art director was half creative problem-solver, half a cost-effective way to conceptualise – and sell – what the visual effects (VFX) in a commercial might look like. Rather than enlist an entire unit of 3D artists to experiment with the look of an ad, one or two art directors could efficiently kick-start that process with research and concept art, often done at the pitch stage.

In two years I must have written close to 50 pitch documents in collaboration with various advertising agencies and production companies. The excitement brought by way of brands such as Audi, Nokia and Electronic Arts was overshadowed entirely by getting to work with the talents of people directing. Hearing the director's vision for a commercial fascinated me. Their written treatment, a five or ten-page document, outlined their interpretation of an ad; where and how it would be shot, who they would cast, what the VFX would entail and so on. In typically no more than 1,000 words these documents described the foundations of a story told in 60 seconds or less: enough time to radically alter how we see a brand or business. Every treatment that landed on my desk became my bedtime reading.

Around 12 months in, I came across an in-house pitch to direct the official cinematic (a type of short film) for a Sony PS3 videogame called *Killzone 2* (2009). It doesn't take much to work out the game's style from the title, but knowing nothing about the game – in fact being somewhat disconnected from the games industry altogether – I made my way into research. It turned out the franchise was huge. Millions of loyal fans worldwide had played the first *Killzone* (2004) game. *Killzone 2* was hugely anticipated. As a technical achievement alone it was up there at the head of its genre.

At a time when The Mill was pushing to expand into videogame trailers, this was a big opportunity. But for whatever reason, I felt this particular treatment was comparatively lacking in vitality. I wasn't sure why: the director was as good as they came. I guess he was spread too thinly. Either way, it was missing that vital sense of being a labour of love. Later that afternoon I went to see the exec producer of the project – to this day one of my favourite colleagues, Alex Webster.

"I've been looking at the *Killzone 2* project ... " I said, bounding into the production department. "The deadline is Monday, but how would you feel if over the weekend I put together a second treatment? I'll work with Ed again, collect our thoughts and do some concept art.

"If you think it's any good," I said to Alex, "submit it to the client. If not – don't."

I often think of this project and appreciate Alex's leap of faith. Our ability to write and direct a game trailer was entirely unsubstantiated, but over that weekend Ed (who was also at The Mill) and I put together a branded treatment with four pieces of concept art and a collection of reference material. On Sunday night I emailed everything to Alex and waited, with no expectation other than a hope he might consider us for similar future projects. It was really a pitch to let us pitch.

On Thursday of the same week Alex told us we had got the job. Our treatment was chosen from all the production companies pitching and we were about to direct an official (and costly) trailer for Sony Computer Entertainment Europe. All thanks to Alex.

The enthusiasm of Arran Green and everyone at Sony helped get us through the early meetings. If the production timeline of *Solar* seemed lengthy, people in the games industry work on a title for two or three years at a time. Enthusiasm is a necessity. Unfortunately, the entire project was later canned higher up the chain at Sony and the budget was pulled. In hindsight we should have done a better job of trying to salvage it – I wouldn't give up a project so easily these days.

Thankfully we got the chance to work with Arran and his team one month later when he hired us to direct the promo for a big upcoming title called *MAG* (2010). This time we enlisted the PS3's online community to participate in a one-of-a-kind trailer. Hundreds of fans submitted compelling battle speeches which we edited into a 120-second voiceover. The result generated PR buzz as one of the most talked about trailers in its genre. In the process, Ed and I got to work with the most fun and talented people at The Mill in the studio department.

There is a fine line between being humbly proactive and waiting for things to find you, but one approach has a much higher success rate than the other. Too many people believe 'If I just do good work, they will find me.' Unfortunately, unless you are very lucky, you may be waiting a long time. The people who are vocal, but not neanderthal or uncivilised, the ones who ask and make their own opportunities – they are the people who get to tell the 'right place, right time' Morecambe and Wise stories.

Alex is the best manager and producer I have ever worked with. He gave us the conditions to achieve something, to surprise ourselves and everyone else, and probably fought like hell for us, just like Tim Lindsay talked about. Great managers create opportunities for those who want them. But had I not asked or showed interest, chances are we wouldn't have registered as anything more than a faint blip on Alex's radar in terms of direction talent.

At this point I think it helps to consider why children have an endless need to inquire. They know what they want and ask if they can have it, and they have no reservations about doing so.

They ask because they don't have an answer. The irony is that, as we get older, we probably still don't have the answer. We just think we do, and it's a negative one, so we don't bother finding out for sure. It's a ridiculous trap.

The process of selling ourselves (and everything it entails) shouldn't suddenly provoke a stigma once we stop being children. In its purest form it is simply saying, 'These are the things I have done, I am proud of them,' or, 'Here is what I want to accomplish'.

You're not entering into some kind of Faustian pact. No apology is necessary.

You and you alone are the driving force behind your career and the things that can be achieved. And the best of us shine the spotlight on others – no one receives enough praise for doing smart, ambitious or honourable things.

4

CURIOSITY AND PURPOSE

"Question everything generally thought to be obvious." — DIETER RAMS

On the ground floor of a building, an engineer is working tirelessly to perfect the combustion engine. He never leaves the house. He is obsessed about the engine, the mechanics of it all: the metallurgy, the electronics, the fuel technology.

This labour of love is an all-consuming quest to reduce revolutions, increase efficiency, generate more power and do so safely with less sound and fewer vibrations. The project has commanded his attention for the better part of a decade.

One day there is an unexpected knock at his door. The man, unfamiliar with interruptions, goes to investigate. Greeting him is a bright-eyed eight-year-old boy. The child has heard the man working on his machine when walking past the building over the last few years. Having noticed things have finally been getting quieter and the workshop sounds more refined, he is interested to see what is happening.

"What are you doing here, mister?" the child asks.

"I'm perfecting an engine ... " says the man, gesturing towards the work area.

The child runs in to inspect the machine.

"It's very impressive! What's it for?"

"What do you mean?"

"Well, you know, what's it for? Engines drive things, don't they?"

Having never left the house, the engineer doesn't understand the question at all. So the child takes him outside to explore, showing him all the things with an engine: cars, aeroplanes, trains and so on.

By all accounts it is an epiphany for the engineer. The following day he decides to build a car. He can't believe how wonderful they are. And he's a smart man, so for this new task he constructs a driving circuit nearby to test the vehicle.

Over time, the car he builds is remarkable. He brings the centre of gravity down, widens the wheelbase and conducts himself with the same unyielding attention to detail as with the engine: improving speed, efficiency, aerodynamics and handling. The car is endlessly going round his circuit, faster and faster. One day the engineer notices someone watching from the edge of the track and walks over to investigate.

"Excuse me," he says. "I've seen you here before. You're staring at me and my work – who are you?"

"Oh, you don't remember me?" replies the stranger. "I met you when I was eight. I'm 16 now. I asked what the purpose was of the engine you were perfecting. I see now you have built an incredible car."

"Ah! Indeed!" says the man, unable to resist a smile. "What do you think?"

"It looks fantastic. What's it for?"

"What do you mean what's it for?"

"Well," said the boy, "cars take journeys ... they take people places, don't they?"

The man looks at the circuit, and the car so perfectly adapted to drive on it and do nothing else, and once again struggles to respond to the boy. In eight years, despite all his efforts, all the painstaking attention to detail, the engineer still hadn't considered the real purpose of what he was doing.

Applied creativity

Michael Wolff, one of the leading authorities on brands, told me this story as a metaphor for the businesses and individuals who are forever tuning their engines without focusing on the destination it will take them. They are working tirelessly – perhaps harder than anyone else – but as long as their efforts are applied without purpose or vision, their potential is limited.

The proper application of creativity is of acute importance right now. It can make our lives profoundly more enjoyable and easier to navigate. It can spark revolutions, change the way we think, define the future and re-tell the past. People whose lives are spent making something from nothing are very, very lucky and the work in which they choose to exercise their imagination is a demonstration of who they are and what they believe about the world around them.

What follows in this chapter is a reminder for you and me that creativity and the entrepreneurial spirit that it's connected to – just like with the engineer and the child – are at their best when *curiosity* impels *purpose*.

And vice versa.

Purpose

If you were to ask a typical business leader what the purpose of their role or organisation is, what do you suppose their answer would be?

On most occasions it would likely include some or all of the following:

"To generate profit, grow the company and reward shareholders."

Nothing unexpected there. And they would argue that those factors make perfect sense, at least in the short term.

What if you were to ask a surgeon the same question? Perhaps their answer would be along the lines of:

"To use the skills and knowledge I have acquired to save and improve lives."

I don't have many surgeon friends but I don't think that's taking too much of a liberty.

The very real contrast here is instructive. The business reply is from the increasingly outdated and obvious model of 20th century business: short-term, profit-motivated and perilously old-fashioned. The surgeon's reply comes from a long-term *belief*. And it is an answer that denotes purpose, rather than outcome.

This kind of reply is what 21st century businesses need to be able to give. In fact, the best are already doing it. Leading entrepreneurs are putting purpose at the core of their work. These people are creating companies and products that attract customers, inspire their staff, solve problems and disrupt industries for the better. Their enduring philosophy creates authentic culture and the company and its individuals keep their spark.

So for creatives the question is: what is the *purpose* of our creativity? What is the purpose of the things we do day-to-day? Of our ambitions?

There are countless creatives and entrepreneurs whose accomplishments are driven by belief and purpose. Sir Richard Branson, one of the world's top business leaders and who is anything *but* typical, runs the Virgin Group this very way. In his own words:

"I can honestly say that I have never gone into any business purely to make money. If that is the sole motive, then I believe you are better off not doing it."

I see no reason to treat creativity any differently to how Sir Richard treats business. In both, the reward of meeting a purpose and fulfilling a belief far outweighs the value of any potential profit. And in fact, focusing on belief and purpose is probably the best way of letting profit take care of itself. It allows you to create a story worth telling. It makes something a labour of love. It usually ends in giving customers something they love almost as much as you do.

One of Sir Richard's companies is Virgin Unite, run by CEO Jean Oelwang. Founded in 2004, the mission of Virgin Unite, as the charitable arm of the Virgin Group, is to explore how they can harness all the creative and entrepreneurial spirit across the group's 80 businesses, their assets in Sir Richard and the Virgin brand, and come together to drive large-scale positive change. By bringing together great ideas and passionate people their wish isn't to save the world, but instead create ways to reinvent how we live and work in it. They want to put people and the planet alongside profit. Jean elaborates ...

JEAN OELWANG: *I started my career in telecommunications and marketing and one day decided I was going to go off and try to do good in the world. I went to work for a homeless shelter for young people in the centre of Chicago and later volunteered at VISTA – a programme similar to the domestic Peace Corps in the US – with homeless teenagers aged between 16 and 21. For me that was probably the first time I realised how screwed up the world was if we were letting these young kids live on the streets. But also how screwed the systems were from the government, business and social sectors.*

When I moved to London, I spent about 18 years helping start-up mobile phone companies. We did that in Bulgaria, Columbia and later South Africa, then ended up in Asia. I went into the non-profit sector and worked for the Foundation for National Parks and Wildlife, and one day got a call from Virgin to help set up a mobile company.

Four or five years later when we'd got the business running, I went to Richard and my board. After working in so many emerging markets I became really passionate about how we can change the way business and the social sector work together. I was lucky at the time that Richard was looking to set up a foundation. I put together a business plan and he said, "Let's do it". Richard has always done a lot in this area. He's had it in his blood since he was a teenager. He was interested in how he can take his 80 businesses, along with the brand, and really leverage a far larger scale of change in the world. We started Virgin Unite together around ten years ago.

Unite is fundamentally about how business can and must be a force for good in the world, how we can put people and the planet alongside profit at the very core of businesses. It's no longer a matter of a box-checking exercise that you have to do. We think it's a matter of businesses surviving going forward.

That's because we think there are three things convening to make this whole movement scale rapidly. One is that businesses don't own brands anymore, people own the brands; and that very transparency is going to force businesses to change. The second thing is that business leaders are now starting to stand up for the first time and in a very significant way, like Paul Polman of Unilever or Jochen Zeitz from Puma, who is now putting in place an environmental profit and loss statement to calculate the value of the natural resources he's utilising. They are starting to show that movement from leadership. The third part of the perfect storm is that we are seeing lots of new competitors coming in, like the Innocent Drinks of this world. Hundreds of new businesses are putting purpose at their centre and are going to be a competitive pressure for existing businesses.

Jean and her team at Virgin Unite currently run hundreds of programmes around the world to help support this new model. They include the Branson Centre for Entrepreneurship, Galactic Unite, which helps support young people going into science, maths and technology; The Carbon War Room, a group of eight entrepreneurs who have come together to look at new approaches to reducing carbon; and The Elders, a collection of independent global leaders working for peace and human rights, founded in 2007 by Nelson Mandela, with support from Virgin Unite.

JEAN: *Out of all of this, what we are really doing is building a community of people who never accept the unacceptable. And that permeates through all that we do. It involves either transforming an existing business, or starting a new business with purpose at the centre. We have seen several incredibly successful businesses prove this. If you look at Marks & Spencer for example, they have saved over £100 million through their 'Plan A' initiative.*

A few examples that match Jean's goals at Unite include an initiative happening right now in the slums of Manila called *A Litre of Light*. Created by Illac Diaz and the MyShelter Foundation, the project originates from a piece of simple design innovation that brings light to otherwise dark interiors deprived of electricity. Using a simple plastic bottle, filled with water then installed into a purpose-cut hole in the tin roofs of people's homes, the eco-friendly device refracts light from the sun into the room below.

This easily replicable 'solar bottle bulb', which generates an equivalent of 50 watts of light, is now providing sustainable energy practices to millions in underprivileged communities nationwide. Simple technology, from innovation with purpose, that grants a greatly improved standard of living for lots of families.

And we can find a similar story in Peace One Day. Film-maker Jeremy Gilley first set out to produce a documentary about the issue of peace and chronicle his campaign to establish an annual day of non-violence. In 1999 Gilley founded the non-profit organisation Peace One Day, whose efforts later inspired the member states of the United Nations to unanimously adopt the first ever day of global ceasefire, 21 September. In 2007 their efforts meant 4.5 million children were able to receive the vaccination for polio.

The essence of these two accomplishments originate from creativity driven by purpose, and we can class both Gilley and

Diaz as successful entrepreneurs as a result. But 'entrepreneur' is a term that can quickly become lost in meaning, even if its role and defining characteristics are as important as ever.

JEAN: *An entrepreneur is someone who starts out by never accepting the unacceptable, he or she is someone who is willing to go out and look at something through a radically different lens. Using Richard as an example, every time I meet with him I'm astonished how he looks at things from a different perspective than anyone I have ever worked with. He never thinks of how you can't do something, he only thinks how you can do something. And that's the beauty of an entrepreneur, they have this unbelievable sense of optimism that they believe they can deliver and can achieve. This is why it's so important to get that entrepreneurial spirit into how we solve problems in the world.*

I don't see it anymore as business, government, social, creative or design sectors. I see all of those silos breaking down, and the beauty of where we're headed in the world right now is seeing the merger of those different sectors. For a young creative person coming in I would recommend they don't put themselves into those silos either, but think about how, as a creative mind, they can help create a new approach, rather than working in an industry and a sector. Creative people who look at how we solve issues and how we reinvent how we live and work in the world are the most important thing right now.

We've screwed things up in the last several decades, we're in a mess and we need a new way of thinking, we need creative people to come in and start saying 'Actually, that's wrong' and constantly questioning things. One of the things Richard always says is that the reason he's continued to build is that he's stayed curious.

Creativity and entrepreneurialism give us joy, discovery and wonder in a thousand forms. They can also make an enormous impact on the world. The point is not that *everyone's* raison d'être should be to set up a non-profit organisation and help impoverished communities, but simply that considering the purpose of the work we do can help deliver results that make the biggest impact.

Even Google's mission statement may surprise you: "*To organise the world's information and make it universally accessible and useful.*" With less vision that could have been stripped down and remained as something like 'sell search-based advertising'. Thankfully Larry Page and Sergey Brin's vision has taken it much further.

In creativity and business alike it is more rewarding and fun to build products, content or services that start with a *why*. To do that we have to ask the right questions, using a child's curiosity to interrogate the status quo.

Curiosity

Michael Wolff is one of the world's leading creative advisors to global corporations and educational institutions. He is co-founder of the iconic design consultancy Wolff Olins, former president of D&AD, visiting professor at the University of the Arts in London, senior fellow at the Royal College of Art and someone who has an inimitable combination of experience and appreciation in the values of creativity and youth.

When we are young, we have an immense natural ability to be receptive. It is when we can most appreciate and be inspired by the intricacies of everything around us. It is also us at our most inquisitive, when we are forever asking questions and yet remain perfectly at ease with the idea of being often wrong. Every answer is another question waiting to happen, and *that's OK.*

It seems a great shame that many people, including Michael, feel these instinctive creative proficiencies are not gratified during those years which are spent in education.

MICHAEL WOLFF: *I didn't understand anything to do with how I was educated. In fact, I didn't enjoy any aspect of the process of education. My life at school was really to do with tribes of one sort or the other, and I was so busy seeking approval that I really didn't bother very much with the subjects.*

I remember going back to school and seeing this grid with vertical and horizontal lines. It had things like 'Maths' and 'English' and whatever written on it, and I just thought of those as 40 minutes of purgatory, really. I was much more interested in looking out of the windows.

And this meant I noticed all sorts of things that seemed to pass my classmates by. I remember my first bicycle and the intensity of its blue paint and the quality of the enamel. I knew that colour was very important and that I really enjoyed it. In fact, all the aesthetic elements of various objects, other than just their look, fascinated me.

They still do.

Consider the miracle of an orange. An orange has an amazing colour. It also has an amazing texture. And you already know what's in it, but it's very secretive. Then there's the process of opening it: there's its incredible structure, then its aroma, then its taste.

How many things do we create that give us such a dramatic sequence of sensual delight compared to picking up and eating an orange? Very few. And yet even then we let ourselves get bored by the process of opening an orange.

It's probably worth taking a moment to re-read the previous couple of paragraphs. It took me a moment to be as grateful as I should be for what Michael said here – it's extraordinary how fast we can lose appreciation of what's around us.

We've lost wonder in all sorts of things. And yet it is that appreciation, that process of consciously noticing, which provides a master-key for unlocking creative potential. Michael believes there to be three 'muscles' of creativity, each of which must be exercised in order to get to that potential. And it all begins with curiosity.

MUSCLE I: CURIOSITY

Curiosity, the uncompromising desire to know or learn something new, is the process of always asking and always questioning. Why is that like that? How does that work? Why does this happen? Why do we think this way? How can this be doing its job better?

It is the step that occurs immediately before a discovery. A great children's fable reads: *"He who asks is a fool for five minutes, but he who doesn't ask is a fool forever"*. Curiosity should remain infinite. Our capacity to learn relies on asking questions and we should never be afraid of our ignorance. To put it another way, as Michael Wolff also told me: "Be suspicious of anyone who thinks they are right."

MUSCLE 2: APPRECIATION

The second muscle is *appreciation*. Well-exercised appreciation allows us to notice the value in everything we encounter. But it is also the process of understanding the sensitivities of people and the ability to step into the shoes of others (or those of a business) and understand who they are and how things work. All while free of assumptions.

This is best illustrated by the true story of designer and gerontologist Patricia Moore. Gerontology is the study of the social, psychological and biological aspects of ageing. At just 26 years old, Patricia Moore, a masters graduate from Columbia University, took to extreme lengths to satisfy her curiosity. Beginning May 1979 and lasting nearly three and a half years, Moore disguised herself as an 85-year-old woman while travelling to 116 cities and towns in 14 states across the United States and Canada.[5]

Her goal was to develop an appreciation of how society and public situations affected the elderly, then apply the information to design better experiences for them. Her transformation into various roles – ranging from wealthy dowager to bag lady – consisted of extensive make-up, fixing splints to her knees to simulate stiffness, wrapping her fingers in tape and covering them in cotton gloves to duplicate the effect of arthritis, plugging her ears to reduce hearing and applying Vaseline under contact lenses to mimic the effects of cataracts. She would assume these guises for 12 hours a day, up to five days a week. The sometimes devastating effects of this research, including permanent damage to her back after being attacked by a gang, led to her developing major new products for the elderly with clients that included 3M, AT&T, General Electric, Herman Miller, Kimberly-Clark, Johnson & Johnson and NASA.

In 1983 she appeared on the *Today* show to talk about her journey and later wrote the book *Disguised: A True Story* (1985). There are a great many people around the world who are are finding their lives easier to navigate thanks to one curious and inspiring woman.

Patricia Moore's work meant she was able to understand almost completely how difficult or even terrifying life can be for the elderly.

---

5   Full interview with Moore available in *People* magazine from June 24, 1985. www.people.com/people/archive/article/0,,20091155,00.html

Illac Diaz showed the same appreciation when he created *A Litre of Light*. The world right now is full of increasingly difficult challenges. But with these challenges come vast opportunities if we only try to appreciate them. Making purposeful creative investments into health, education, resources, or the ageing population, will make a serious impact. They require stories that people will want to hear and products that people will want to use.

History shows us that the ideas that make a big impact often start at grassroots level. Perhaps it is no wonder. It wasn't a government body or pharmaceutical conglomerate that did Patricia Moore's research. It was one passionate individual. For most large organisations, that kind of approach would be like changing the engines on the aeroplane while it's in the air. That's why today is such an exciting time for those who want to change things.

JEAN: *Industries are being transformed right now. We're just seeing the tip of the iceberg. If you're in a rural place in Africa, a doctor can download the latest thinking on a response to a specific disease right to their mobile. The interesting thing is we already have a lot of the technologies needed for this. It's just that we haven't really listened to people on the front lines to better understand how we apply it.*

I experienced a huge turning point in South Africa. We were about to launch one of the first prepaid services in that country in the mid-90s and we went to hundreds of market research agencies who all said "Don't do it, you're not going to have any customers". Within the first month we'd hit our annual sales target.

So we went into the townships and what we quickly saw is that people had taken the phones and adapted them for their own purposes. It was radically transforming their small businesses and our business was booming because of it. This kind of thing convinces me that by just going out and listening and understanding what people need, a lot of the technology that we currently have could be creating plenty of development solutions already.

MUSCLE 3: IMAGINATION

When we are able to realise what isn't working and what can be done to solve it, that's when we get the most value out of our imagination, the final muscle in the chain. And only when the previous two – curiosity and appreciation – are connected is there sufficient strength to exercise it. When we have all three working together we should allow absolutely nothing to stop them. We should only dare to fail.

As I listened to Michael Wolff, surrounded by Eames furniture and one-of-a-kind artwork in his faultlessly designed home, I sat taking notes. Important though they were to me, these notes were written with no particular ostentation. They were made with the same black rollerball pen I always write with, in the same kind of Moleskine workbook I always carry with me. I highlighted headings the same way, drew the same kind of arrows to make connections between entries and dated the page in the top-righthand corner like I always do.

My method of adding things in this book and all those I have filled hasn't changed in the last five years. It is a process I go through often – usually with hope of a useful outcome – and it's based entirely on habit.

The same can be said for most of the seemingly trivial things I do daily; the route I take to work, where I hang my coat, where I buy food, what music I listen to, what time I go to the gym. Even some of the brief real-life interactions I have with people can become routine over time.

All these habits are quantifiable, minimise unpredictability and generally don't much impede the important things I want to devote the bulk of my attention to. In other words, they are a pretty safe and uninspired way to make decisions. I'm not necessarily aware of them all, and I'm sure I'm not alone, but what worries me is what else this is being applied to. Why would that be a problem? Because habit can mean a defeat of purpose and curiosity.

It's always a good idea to ask ourselves how much we rely on our assumptions. How often do we have an automatic reaction to a problem that needs solving? How frequently do we give unconditional value to something merely because of comfortable past standards?

It's not always a cause for concern but we do this kind of thing in every aspect of our lives. "We never change the way we walk, because we never think to change the way we walk," as Michael pointed out. Walking isn't necessarily something that we need to radically innovate in each year, no matter how entertaining, but realising the outcome of an action is being defined by habit, and taking action to change it, can be highly advantageous. Especially when that action is exercising creativity.

Any work which is predicated on the habits or assumptions we build up over time can have greatly limited potential. Assumptions are often outdated or broken, or both, and they can do an injustice to our true capabilities. Hanging on to opinions or relying on habits in creativity can lead to repetition, blinkered vision and rigid process – three of the things that starve innovation. Yet to overcome the ones that might hold us back, all we have to do is become aware they exist and challenge them. Discovery is more likely to occur if we are willing to walk a little differently (figuratively speaking).

Not that it's always easy. Like many company leaders, Michael witnessed something like a reliance on habits begin to happen as his firm Wolff Olins matured. Fighting that reliance is the only way to keep on making something new. But doing so can come at a cost.

MICHAEL: *The board saw someone who was dangerous. Someone who was inconsistent with the idea of process. I was definitely disruptive, and remained disruptive. I actually regard disruptiveness as a very useful aspect of living. I don't think any of us at that time saw the purpose of it to the business. I think I started to be interested in it, but I didn't see it. Nor did they.*

Infuriate a handful of people and you're probably doing something right. But ultimately Michael's vigilance towards process resulted in him leaving Wolff Olins on terms he described to me as "at the end of their feet".

Of course, you could argue Michael's desire to be disruptive itself became habitual over time. And that is a real risk: like anything, if it becomes at all unquestioning, there is a risk of stagnation. The key is being aware enough to detect even that.

Challenging the habits that expand as companies and individuals grow is scary and uncertain. But diversity, rather than conformity, is what makes us thrive. It is a more difficult sell than sticking to the obvious and the status quo. But successful creatives and entrepreneurs are not the kind of people to let that bother them.

If we are right there with the engineer, facing our challenge, we should also make sure to be the child who questions it all – just enough – so there's purpose.

5

LEARN FOREVER
AND PLAY

"For the love of God, son, whatever you do, don't be a lawyer."

— ALAN WHARTON (RETIRED LAWYER)

One of the most legendary blues guitarists was once asked, "How long did it take you to learn the guitar?"

He paused for a moment. Then smiled and replied, "I'll let you know when I've learned."

This chapter aims to show just how great an answer that was.

No expert

In early 2012 I was invited to speak for the first time at a McKinsey & Company summit in Stockholm. McKinsey is a global management consulting firm that helps the world's leading businesses, governments and institutions make lasting and substantial improvements in their performance. Their insights, which serve two-thirds of the Fortune 500, are kept unequalled by investing significant time and effort in developing their knowledge. This happens within their 18 industry practices, eight functional practices and the McKinsey Institute. In short, they are world-class problem-solvers.

The summit was held for the firm's Telecoms, Media and Technology practice, and I was billed to share insights on the future of the mobile industry. For years up to this point I had spoken at universities and conferences on creativity or how media was changing. But never before had I faced an upcoming talk with such a keen sense of my own absolute uselessness. Giving advice to McKinsey felt comparable to calling up Sir Tim Berners-Lee and offering web tech support:

"Have you tried turning it off and on again, Tim?"

As an organisation, McKinsey had never struck me as one that operated much on uncertainty, so during the outbound flight to Stockholm-Arlanda airport I saw I had two options for how my session at the conference could be conducted.

One, I could try to be the expert the role required, where my heavy-handed vernacular and industry jargon implied I had all the important answers in an attempt to save face and live up to expectations.

Or the less-favoured option two: stand in a room filled with people of appreciably greater intellect and say simply and truthfully that I, in fact, didn't have many answers about the future of the industry. It would be admitting to some very smart people that there are gaps in my knowledge.

It was an uncomfortable situation; neither option seemed good.

The behavioural relevance is that the internal conflict as to how I would conduct myself originated entirely from a broken definition of the term 'expert'. Of course, on paper, I know this shouldn't have been a decision that needed making, and it's nowhere near good enough to think I hesitated.

My perception that the audience in Stockholm would already know everything they could possibly need to, thereby making option one the more appealing choice (skate over things to maintain my aura of expertise, rather than plunge into the unknown), did them no justice whatsoever. That's precisely *not* the attitude that has helped McKinsey lead an industry since the 1920s.

Thankfully, I chose option two.

Fortunately there was fairly immediate proof we are always better rewarded by following the uninhibited approach. Before long the forum turned into an open discussion with many of the delegates on how certain mobile strategies, financial and business models may or may not be relevant for their clients. If anything, we all left that day with more questions than answers, but it was far more valuable to spend time actually learning from one another than the alternative of my pride starving the conversation.

But it's tough. Sometimes the instinct is to believe the opposite is more rewarding. When do we ever want to risk looking like we're not the sure-thing? That we don't have all the answers, or know all there is to know? We spend so much time investing so heavily in our self-image that the risk of drawing attention to a weakness feels too dangerous.

And all the while, we all know that what's most beneficial is candour and humility in knowing there is plenty still to be learned or figured out – no matter the circumstances. The ability to learn does not decline with experience, even if learning new things can start to feel like an unrewarding pursuit as we become more expert at something. Just remember the story of Georges St-Pierre and his desire to learn from his fans' fitness challenges. Unfortunately, while I chose correctly at McKinsey, I was less successful during a film shoot in Montréal with Georges. We had a crew of 23 people for two days in one location and there were endless things I have never seen done before. Shoot efficiency was vital, we had to film and photograph Georges performing over 500 exercises for the training product *Touchfit*, with zero contingency on time. As a result, the data wrangler (person in charge of capturing all the footage onto hard-disks) had a method for keeping track of cameras that fascinated me, and the director of photography was using lenses I hadn't ever come across. The majority of me was desperate to ask them to explain all the things I didn't fully understand, but the Ian that was supposedly creatively leading the shoot, and from the company paying for it all, said, *"You should really look like you know that already,"* and won the argument.

So I didn't ask, and now I won't know.

The A-lister in making

When we meet someone or hear stories of someone successful – or come across an organisation at the top of its game – it's easy to see a premium product. The 'final thing'. What is more difficult to do is to picture that company as a two-person start-up sharing office space, with no customers and thread-bare finances.

We become oblivious to the fact that perhaps successful people are *still* figuring everything out just as much as the next person, or that they go through the same process of learning.

Take Bradley Cooper as an example – Hollywood A-List actor, star of *Silver Linings Playbook* (2012) and *The Hangover* trilogy (2009–13). Do you think of him as anything other than the leading man he is today? Such are the mechanics of becoming renowned. People like Cooper emerge to the majority of us only when they're at the top. The process of getting there – and remaining there – is either camouflaged or forgotten.

Inside the Actors Studio is a televised series of seminars from the Actors Studio at Pace University, New York City. The show brings successful movie and television stars in front of a class of acting students where they are interviewed by host James Lipton, followed by a selection of questions from the audience. In January 1999 the show welcomed Sean Penn as one of its long line of famous guests. When it came time for Q&A, as the camera cut to the audience, Penn fielded a question from none other than a young second-year student by the name of Bradley Cooper.

Far removed from red carpets, *Variety* magazine and appearances on *The Tonight Show*, Cooper is there as a student, listening, learning and being inspired by successful actors and film-makers. He can even be seen in other footage from sessions with Robert De Niro and Steven Spielberg. Twelve years later, in March 2011, Cooper was the first graduate of the Actors Studio to be invited back as an interviewee. When asked by one of the audience members what challenges him the most, he responded by saying:

> *"I just want to get better. That's basically what it is, I really just want to keep getting better and better and better – and work harder, and learn [more]. There's literally no difference in my mindset from when I was a student. Zero."*[6]

Part of youthful thinking is to remind ourselves that we are always developing our talents. And that's a life-long pursuit: it's dangerous to assume there's a final version of ourselves on the horizon, and unrealistic to think anyone else is any different. We are never finished and the possibilities are endless. Much more exciting.

---

6   *Inside the Actors Studio*. Series 17, Episode 1. **www.imdb.com/title/tt1804001**

Bradley Cooper, McKinsey, the blues guitarist – they all know it. The most successful people in the world never think their education is over.

Educated mess

So where and how do we pick the sources to learn from, and how do we facilitate the conditions for meaningful learning? How do we attain that measure of clarity and perspective, big or small, which provides us with the understanding to excel beyond what we believe to be our ability? We have to discern the most relevant guidance from family, peers, teachers and colleagues, and leap back and forth between direct influence and the wisdom of people or stories that go beyond everyday life.

Sadly for higher education – one obvious source of meaningful learning – there has never been an easier time to question its value when it comes to creativity.

Part of the problem stems from government decisions which dramatically misalign the need to nurture creativity in relation to economic growth. In fact, creativity rarely figures at all. In 2012 the British government attempted to launch a new academic recognition called the English Baccalaureate (EBacc). The government proposed that schools in England and Wales award EBacc certificates for attainments in five academic pillars: English, maths, sciences, languages and the humanities (history or geography). Incredibly, there was no requirement for the arts to be taught alongside this. Only following sharp opposition by the creative industry, led by Sir James Dyson, did the government perform a U-turn. However the scars from the intent remain.

Other policy problems are numerous, among them rising university fees, funding cuts to the Arts Council and closure of organisations such as the UK Film Council – an organisation whose sole purpose was to promote, educate and fund the country's film industry.

The rise of dropout entrepreneur superstars – Mark Zuckerberg et al. – while a very encouraging phenomenon, is also something of a nail in higher education's coffin for creatives. *If they didn't need university, why do I?* That's the question many young people are asking. And I'm not sure enough institutions are doing a great job of answering it convincingly yet.

A renaissance in higher education's contribution to creativity is possible, but it will take serious determination across the sector. In many ways it cannot wait: the future of the economy relies on a creatively capable and well-informed youth. In the UK alone, the creative economy accounts for around 10% of the country's GVA (gross value added – GDP before subsidies are subtracted) and employs 2.5 million people – more than the financial services, advanced manufacturing and construction industries.[7]

At this moment in time there are several, sometimes conflicting, ideologies about how education reform can help maintain or improve it. But I believe that to reframe the image of creative education will, in part, require educational institutions to simply be as agile as the companies led by the very entrepreneurs who didn't require them in the first place.

Amongst other things, this means:

---

7   Nesta. *Manifesto for the Creative Economy.* **www.nesta.org.uk/library/ documents/A-Manifesto-for-the-Creative-Economy-April13.pdf**

- being capable of iteration and fast change when something doesn't work, as opposed to relying on – and being handicapped by – the curricula commonly seen in undergraduate courses with three-year review cycles

- being first and foremost personalised to each student, rather than standardised – at high school I still remember not being permitted to study both music *and* art because someone universally deemed one arts subject to be 'enough'. These decisions should be made with the individual, not at population level

- an emphasis on teachers being mentors and role models, rather than administrators issuing and grading exams. Creative people are for the most part never more than a few minutes away from a nervous breakdown – a champion is always required. As the saying goes: a successful person is a dreamer who someone believed in

- learning that is playful: in other words, collaborative and explorative, and not short-sighted in its prescribing of skill, but instead a focus on thinking that is future-proofed.

Modern-day village elders

One of the most relevant and yet rare models for creative learning is London's School of Communication Arts, a world-leading advertising school led by dean Marc Lewis. The SCA condenses three years' worth of learning into a single year and guarantees work placements for all students, or up to £10,000 from an investment fund to start a business after graduation. Alumni are regularly honoured by top industry awards and hired by the very best creative agencies around the world.

What makes the school's programme so meaningful is a qualification not written by academics with a three-year review cycle, but instead by an always-relevant collaboration with the industry – formed around mentoring.

As students work on live briefs throughout the year, they are supported by hundreds of leading mentors from all manner of industries and disciplines. I have attended days where an advertising legend is mentoring alongside an ex-physicist, a designer and a business author. The students at SCA have a very real appetite for broad learning and are given the ideal environment to indulge it – including a masterclass I witnessed from Hermann Hirschberger, an 86-year-old Holocaust survivor, to help the class with a brief for the London Jewish Cultural Centre.

The diversity of mentors and the innovative open-source wiki model for its learning is what makes the school so nimble and its students so successful. And if we are to have any richness or variety in our thinking, like students at the SCA we need to take our learning from different perspectives. One of the students, Jack Cooney, told me:

"Having regular mentors eliminates the barriers that a formal education usually creates. The status quo of education cannot teach you what the SCA model does. You gain incredible insights into the world that you want to be a part of by having daily one-on-ones with

people who are in the industry right now. I'm not afraid of entering a 'big bad world' once school finishes."

That's what good mentors do: they arm us with the self-belief and knowledge that makes the 'big bad world' no big deal. And if young people are turning away from higher education – for which many wouldn't blame them – it falls firmly at the feet of the industries who need them to make the investment in the meantime.

Someone who is taking part of that challenge on is Emma Sexton, director at SheSays, a global organisation running free mentorship and networking events for over 3,000 women in the creative industries.

EMMA SEXTON: *A mentor is the modern-day village elder, sharing life experience and knowledge with their community. They might be a manager, a colleague or a friend-of-a-friend. What's important is that the mentor can share and offer advice that is of value.*

Mentoring is so important for a successful career. There is often the assumption that a mentor is only needed when you are younger and just starting out. But mentoring is even more crucial as your career develops and you move onto more challenging roles and leadership positions.

Whilst a mentor may have vast amounts of experience and knowledge that they are keen to share, they should not push a mentee into doing exactly what they might have done. It is not about creating a 'mini-me', but about nurturing and helping the mentee to develop and discover the right path for them. The mentor is the provider of a much bigger picture. A mistake that many people make is that they are reluctant to ask somebody to become their mentor.

We will later hear Jamie Oliver tell how fashion designer and mentor, Paul Smith, influenced his work. For me, three people have contributed to my career as mentors: Theresa O'Brien – who lit a fire while teaching me graphic design at college; Jon Lander – creative director at the first agency that employed me; and Ajaz Ahmed.

Individually their input has been very different, but collectively they all share the same single characteristic: they are all people that have my respect. Mentors must above all be someone whose opinion we value and trust – like my father, whose quote began this chapter. As a former lawyer who knew me well, he was perfectly qualified to suggest law wouldn't be right for me.

As long as the feedback you get is authentic, unbiased and trustworthy, support from a mentor is vital. After three months at the agency where I first worked, Jon Lander gave me two pitches to try and win the accounts of *New Scientist* magazine and Bentley cars. Two big accounts, entrusted to the most junior creative at the agency.

To him, this might not have been much. For me, it kick-started a career and set my trajectory for the next three years. He could have taken the pitches on himself or given them to a more senior member of the team, but he didn't. He wasn't protective of his own value or dismissive of mine, and made it matter-of-fact that I was capable and his support was there if needed – mostly through seemingly small gestures, which with the help of hindsight I now appreciate far more.

Like Jon, great mentors offer us the first chance of finding something out. They make it known there are always open channels for communication and stay approachable and humble, even if the relationship is never formally defined. They teach not by telling us what we should do, or what they would do, but instead by providing the conditions for discovery and asking the right questions for us to find our own answer. They are always impartial, consistent, and at no point hold themselves above others by ensuring it is a dialogue of equals.

People who are unwilling to stay coachable or learn from others will quickly lose relevance in their world and find it a lonely place at the top. If they make it that far. The most successful people know it's better to surround themselves with people they admire, rather than people who admire them, and stay aware enough to learn how to provide these conditions without anything required in return.

There is an assumption that creative people, entrepreneurial people, will find their way regardless, but that needn't and shouldn't be the case. Great things happen when self-worth is set aside to consider the potential of others, and when instead of trying to guess the answer, we ask for help.

Play

One of the greatest innovations in learning emerged in the 19th century from German educator Friedrich Fröbel. His creation of kindergarten, and the idea of discovery through play, recognised that all children have unique abilities and are best nurtured by providing conditions of playfulness to stumble onto things and make meaningful social connections. Fröbel believed that by engaging with the world freely and without expectation, a better understanding of it will occur. His ideas of education reform are still among the most influential and much of his thinking remains in use today.

Beyond kindergarten or pre-school, it's difficult to convince people that play is a good thing. Even creative people who *know* it's a good thing, forget that it's a good thing. And how often do we hear inventors speak of their work as play? Or of the very unserious nature of Silicon Valley – the single most effective centre of innovation the world has seen, at least from an economic perspective?

The question isn't if there *might* be a relationship between the playful reputation of Silicon Valley and its creative output, but whether we want to allow room for it in our work to enjoy the same sort of impact. Incorporating playfulness in business facilitates the best parts of creativity. It also has a positive impact on company culture and how teams are motivated to make the best and most efficient work possible by enjoying what they do.

IDEO, run by chief executive Tim Brown, is an international design and innovation consultancy headquartered in Palo Alto, California. Founded in 1991, the firm now employs over 500 people across offices in New York, London, Tokyo, and San Francisco. IDEO is ranked as one of the most innovative companies in the world, one of *Fortune* magazine's most-favoured employers by MBA students, and has been awarded the Smithsonian Cooper-Hewitt, National Design Museum's National Design Award for Product Design.

TIM BROWN: *We started off initially as an industrial design company but broadened out to apply design innovation to as many different fields as we can impatiently get our hands on. Now that ranges from products to services, software, hardware, experiences for brands, and we occasionally wander into the world of marketing and communication. We work for large companies, start-ups and more and* more for governments, foundations and NGOs, covering pretty much the broad business, civic and social sectors.

Play is not the opposite of work. Play is the opposite of stupid. It is discovery-based learning. And if you define it that way, then it's obvious it has a role in creativity because creativity is essentially about discovery.

At IDEO we have a series of more or less effective ways of achieving that, as play is a very broad set of activities. When you watch kids, they have role play, constructive play and competitive play – there are many kinds. So there are many ways of applying play to the creative process. We don't use all of them, but we certainly use quite a few of them.

We don't necessarily sit down and say, "OK, now we're going to play", but when you take something like prototyping, which is absolutely at the core of what we do, the idea of building to learn – to make something in order to discover how that something should be – there's this myth in the world of creativity that you make the thing after you've already decided how it's going to be. And that's bullshit.

Really, you make something which is often a pale, early notion of what you think it might be, then you make it again, and again. That is a process of play. It's like building with LEGO. In fact, we often use toys like LEGO to make early prototypes, because it's fast and it's easy. It's not like we're sitting there thinking, "Oh, we're playing now", it's just that we happen to be using its tools.

Role play is another good example when it comes to prototyping. It's an approach we use all the time, particularly when designing a game or a service. If we are trying to solve a problem for a particular scenario, we often use role play to act out how we think something is going to be. When kids use role play, to become an astronaut or nurse or whatever, they are projecting themselves into a world because it allows them to learn about it. It also allows them to explore it in a safe way. And we need to do that all the time.

Look at the biographies of all of the people who are truly creative – not just in art, but in science, politics and wider fields. You can see how they were playful, how they were curious and how they discovered things in the world. It was not from sitting at a desk doing a nine-to-five job, or by doing the same thing every day. Intellectual curiosity and play are very closely linked.

One of the things about Bill Moggridge, one of the IDEO founders, that just oozed out of him, was his playful discovery. He was a humorous and playful person, and it caused him to be curious about everything. He wouldn't make big assumptions, he'd go and find out. That led him to make some really important discoveries as a designer. And he was insistent that inspiration came from being out in the world, not being sat at your desk trying to pull it out of your brain. You have to put something in there first. How do you do that if you're chained to a desk all day?

Distractingly good ideas

We need to work hard. Increasingly so. There is no great achievement or success in life without serious effort. Innovation is tough, people only want to hire or collaborate with people who give *everything* they have. And great ideas never come to fruition on their own.

Needless to say, granting serious energy to our work is undeniably one of the most important things we can do. If we don't do it ourselves, someone, somewhere else is going to. And they will be the ones who succeed.

Nevertheless, when the operational norm switches to every waking hour spent trying to run at full-throttle, greater damage than good results. It's a state of affairs that is vastly inconsistent with engaging creative potential. And deep down we all know it.

Happily, play can also cover those important moments when the mind is allowed to whir down to a delicate idle. It is important to let our minds relax when necessary, and to spend time not necessarily intending to be creative. Plenty of successful creatives and business leaders have a staggering dedication to their work, interwoven with moments of profound laziness. The result is still one of seemingly inhuman output

There is a reason for this, as Tim Brown theorises ...

TIM BROWN: *I don't know how much deep scientific research there is on this, but I'm fairly convinced that people have good ideas almost at the moment when their brains are distracted rather than focused on the main thing.*

Going off at the weekend and doing some tough hike, or going skiing, or something which is nothing to do with what you'd normally be doing, you come back and your mind is in a fresh state because it's been relaxed.

At IDEO we try and remember that play also has a role in the parts of the job that are seen as the implementation stages, which is often lots and lots of hard work. Traditionally when our project teams are done with a project, they'll have some sort of playful celebration which includes constructing some ridiculous project award for all the team out of something that has an amusing reference to the project.

That doesn't have any particular purpose, but it helps the team reach closure. Ultimately, if you want creative people – who are often impatient and want to move on to the next thing – to apply themselves for a long period of time implementing something they have come up with, you have to find ways of making it fun for them.

Importantly, play almost always has some rules associated with it. It's not chaos, it's not entropy, it's not anarchy. Sometimes those rules are established by the physical materials, like LEGO. The rules of playing with LEGO are established by those modules and the way they click together. Whereas with the rules of role play, many kids don't know explicitly what the rules are, but they learn that you have a better role play if you are being empathic to what the other person is acting out and you build off that. You don't stand there arguing about whether or not they are a good astronaut, you accept it and build from it. And they turn out to be the rules of improvisation.

In order to create these specific moments of play, there has to be a culture that allows room for them. Exercising creativity demands a leap of faith and has two possible outcomes:

- we discover something that has value and the gamble pays off

- we have an idea that excites us enormously, gets explored further, and makes fools of us when it turns out to be nonsense.

So facilitating the leap of faith requires a culture where people aren't afraid to look a bit stupid. That means trust. And a playful culture is one which encourages that trust.

Digital design studio ustwo, cofounded by Matt 'Mills' Miller, has found a very accessible way to translate this into their business. Where many companies run the risk of creating an *appearance* of a playful culture by having some of its bold artefacts in place, like foosball tables or slides installed in the lobby, and then wrongly assume their teams will automatically become creative, ustwo achieve it through an accumulation of smaller but authentic and meaningful gestures. It's in their DNA. The atmosphere and energy as you walk around the ustwo studio is unlike that of any company I have visited.

MILLS: *We founded ustwo in late 2004 in a kitchen with the help of a £5,000 family loan to buy two laptops and keep us going for a couple of months. Our mission was to build a studio where like-minded creatives could share unique ideas and ultimately bring them to life.*

So we set about creating an environment that we looked forward to coming to each day. Our business was about being creative with technology, and this meant we found ourselves in a fast-moving industry where we could make a difference. Our first client was Sony Ericsson. As a company they encouraged flexibility throughout the working environment, and so did we.

Like a lot of design companies that are run by 'creative types', it goes without saying that if you enjoy the space you work in, chances are your people will thrive there. So from day one our company culture has always been our bedrock and has been crucial to our success. We have something unique, and it comes from the simple notion that as founders and best friends, we wanted to build a company that wasn't all about work, but instead about life, passion and play.

We firmly believe that environment directly relates to this culture, so if you hire the right talent, create the right environment, then you are two-thirds of the way there. The only remaining component is getting the right work through the doors.

When you spend at least nine hours a day in a studio, it's fundamental that we make the experience as perfect as possible for each person's needs. We believe the workplace should be as welcoming as a front room and feel like home – and we've personally built the studio from the heart up. We've consciously created a space that blurs the boundaries between work and home life. Our aim is for our people to feel more excited about a Sunday evening than a Friday night, because if they are doing what they love and having fun, they shouldn't want to escape it.

As we've become more successful it's allowed us to invest in our team more and more. We make sure we purchase laptops over desktops for mobility purposes, something in the early days that wasn't possible. We have a lot of space in our studio with numerous break-out areas, meeting rooms for private or open discussions, a 24-hour stocked beer fridge and an open-plan kitchen where everyone is encouraged to socialise, with a barista-grade coffee machine at the centre of it all.

Throughout the studio we use a Sonos music system, intended to give control directly to those who enjoy listening to music. Every zone of the studio is controlled by the Sonos app and any member of the team can change the music. It's their space and the only rule we have is ... there must be music. We've even gone one stage further and created our own desktop application called 'Party Pooper', that allows anyone in the studio to 'thumbs up' or ' thumbs down' certain songs. If enough people disapprove, the music selection moves on – it's a true democracy.

Other services like Instagram and Twitter are an integral part of studio life and we actively pull in everyone's feeds into one stream and promote it to the team via web-based dashboards built into our very own propriety time-tracking software.

As we've grown we've evolved in so many areas of business. Not only has our space expanded but our working approach to clients and projects has done so along with it. We try to group teams next to each other and provide ample space for workshops and regular meetings. We feel clients want to be part of an experience, they want to feel involved with their projects and work with truly engaged people. Our clients want to walk into our studio and be knocked down with an air of excitement.

Work has never been about client and creator but a collaboration between two groups with one unified vision. By creating a positive, collaborative atmosphere, our clients feel at home. Our staff feel at home. I think other industries have a long way to go to get the best from their people.

For ustwo, an open and collaborative culture is how they maximise the creative potential of their team. The results speak on behalf of their commitment. From the years 2011 to 2012, their revenues grew from £7.8m to £10.4m, an increase of 33%. They continued to spend 10% of those revenues on their own intellectual property, which in terms of internal hours, marketing and studio overhead allocation, amounts to over £1m of investment in their team. They also recently launched a dedicated games studio.

All of these actions re-ignite the passion and joy of the ustwo family, and for a company that doesn't take itself too seriously, it has had a serious impact on its industry.

When desire dies

As far as I'm concerned, the ideas in this chapter saved my career. The most fulfilling work we do is centred around learning and play. It's just very easy to forget what that kind of work feels like. That's what companies such as IDEO and ustwo understand, and why they actively cultivate solutions. And forgetting it is why I got into such trouble.

Roughly four years ago I had a senior role in a company that a lot of people would probably have fought me for. I had a good salary, endless possibilities for clients, and was surrounded by hundreds of highly skilled and passionate people. All the right components were in place ... but I had become strained, listless and exhausted. Overwork wasn't the problem. It was a complete lack of desire to continue what I was doing.

I had a burnt-out, laboured mind that was performing to a tenth of its potential. And a worrying realisation struck me – I didn't have any idea how to fix it.

On an evening in April 2009 I met with Michael Maher and Tristan Celder at The Hospital Club in Covent Garden. They told me their story of how they had both left their jobs, founded a technology start-up called Zolmo and needed a designer for a planned joint-venture with Jamie Oliver. The project, a mobile app called *20 Minute Meals*, was a brave leap into an industry so young it would be nearly impossible to model how the end result might fare.

They had a product idea that intended not simply to re-purpose a genre (the cookbook) from legacy, but reinvent it for the digital age. None of us had any experience in mobile and there was no guarantee we could pull it off. I can sit here, take my mind back to that very moment in Covent Garden, and remember the fire and the excitement from this conversation. I was onboard there and then.

Over the next five months, I continued in my day job, but left the agency every day at 7pm and started a night shift working with Michael and Tristan. The scale of the project and commitment it required quickly became clear. From content creation to the technology and design, through to the minefield of pricing and marketing of a digital product: it was challenging, consuming work.

But it was also an entire process that in one way or another was enveloped in serious play. Every week we were each willing to learn dozens of new things, take on new roles and put every ounce of love and joy into the product. On 30 September 2009 we submitted *20 Minute Meals* to the Apple iOS app store. The following year it became a globally top-grossing product, generating over seven figures in revenue, recognised by Apple for 'outstanding design and innovation', featured in their commercials on both sides of the Atlantic and formed a benchmark for all non-game apps to come. *Wired* later wrote how Jamie had "conquered the app store".

Working on *20 Minute Meals* reminded me of three things.

One, that it is entirely possible and occasionally very worthwhile to work around the clock, but only with a non-negotiable clause: to commit those precious extra hours to something that maddeningly excites you through play, and nothing else.

Two, that the problem with my day job was an unfulfilled hunger to learn new things. I had got complacent, and to the agency I was far too valuable as a singularly defined asset for them to risk my time being offered on unknowns.

And three, that over the long haul, when the former two elements (play and desire to learn) are missing in work, what we're doing very quickly ceases to be a labour of love. And when that happens, there's absolutely no chance that what we create will live up to our true potential.

6

DARE TO FAIL

"Creativity is just being stupid enough to not realise that you can't do something."

— GARETH EDWARDS

Gareth Edwards worked as a freelance visual effects artist for the documentaries department of the BBC. But that's not exactly how he put it; in fact, he described himself as "a film-maker pretending to be a visual effects person".[8] His goal was to direct feature films.

Unfortunately, when he told producers and colleagues that he wanted to start directing, no one took him seriously. Everyone simply viewed him as a visual effects artist who had a foolish fantasy he could make films.

After earning a reputation for making £100,000 productions look like they cost double the amount, Edwards had become a valuable and Emmy-nominated asset, not without financial incentive to continue in his current role. But he was also completely sidetracked. So it got to the point where he asked himself how badly he wanted to make films:

"It came right down to the wire of how badly I wanted it. I had wanted to do it since I was so young, I wanted to do it stupidly badly. You get to a point where it's like 'I'd feel better with myself completely failing than I would never having tried,' so you just give it a go."

---

8   Full interview with Edwards on *Collider*: collider.com/gareth-edwards-exclusive-interview-monsters. Additional material from *Daily Telegraph* article: www.telegraph.co.uk/culture/film/filmmakersonfilm/8139791/Gareth-Edwards-interview-loving-the-alien.html

In 2010, with backing from British film and distribution company Vertigo Films, Edwards took a skeleton crew of four people, including himself behind the camera, a cast of two actors, and travelled across Mexico, Belize, Guatemala and Texas to shoot his first feature film *Monsters* (2010).

Created on a micro budget, Edwards filmed with an improvised script and a consumer-grade digital camera. He persuaded locals to get involved as additional actors, had an editor working on location with a £700 laptop, and created all visual effects shots himself from a bedroom.

Monsters was later screened at Cannes Film Festival to wide acclaim, won three British Independent Film Awards and was nominated by BAFTA for Outstanding Début by a British Writer, Director or Producer. At the time of writing (July 2013), Edwards is halfway through shooting the Hollywood re-boot of *Godzilla* for Warner Brothers and Legendary Pictures, set for release in 2014. He has since been dubbed "a filmmaking force to be reckoned with".

This book began with a simple proposal: if you have an idea for an audience, there is nothing, *absolutely nothing*, to stop you from reaching them. Gareth Edwards and his sci-fi road movie *Monsters* is proof of that.

And this chapter covers perhaps the most critical part of the equation. In fact, nothing in the previous five chapters will mean anything at all without this chapter. Until an idea, a passion, a desire to make or do something – in whatever form – is put into practice, it has zero value. Imagination is only ever the beginning of the story.

Anytime I meet with a group of creative people to talk about careers or the industry, I ask the following two questions:

1. *"How many of you at some point have been struck by a great idea that you felt had to be pursued?"*

Slowly but surely, around 90% of people raise their hand.

2. *"How many of you, for whatever reason, never fully saw that idea through to execution?"*

Slowly, but surely, the very same hands are raised once more.

As is mine.

The results are the same between groups of students or seasoned professionals, regardless of industry. And every time, we are always as bemused as everyone else to admit it.

This chapter is not about celebrating failure. There is nothing celebratory about it. And despite a bizarre social shift of doing exactly that, especially in start-up tell-alls and technology confessionals, history is not written by people who only failed all the time. This chapter is a reminder to look differently at the most common reason why those ideas never happened: succumbing to *fear of failure*.

The truth about failure

Creative people have an obligation to put their ideas into practice. Young creatives in particular. Fresh perspectives that challenge the way things are, result in breakthroughs and evolution. But creativity cannot happen if we are afraid.

To be successful, the scary and the challenging have to be faced – which is why we love the story of a hero. Heroes, both real and fictional, are never perfect. They have flaws and get things wrong. They have moments of being down-and-out, but brawl their way back to accomplish something great.

Similarly, if a child isn't sure of the possible result of their actions, they will try it anyway. They too will dare to fail. They don't care about being unsuccessful or looking foolish, to them having a go is part of the fun.

In the process of growing up, we start to condemn mistakes. Too often when groups of people carry out work that is deemed a failure, they are publicly hauled over the coals. We become so aware of situations where we might fail and the repercussions if we do, we stop having a go. American inventor and businessman Charles F. Kettering said in reference to the Wright Brothers, who made powered human flight possible against all the odds and critics, that they "flew right through the smoke-screen of impossibility". The reasons we give ourselves for those raised hands are exactly that, the smoke screen of impossibility.

So why do we fear failure? In a professional capacity there is concern that failure will irreparably tarnish a reputation. This particularly afflicts the successful. The more they are considered a superstar, the more pressure there is to deliver next time. The term 'difficult second album' exists for a reason.

Equally, when we are approached to solve a problem outside our comfort zone, our immediate thought can be, 'I'm not 100% sure of my ability here, and if I screw it up the reputation I have built thus far will be ruined.'

But all this fear really lacks perspective. As long as we keep moving forward, failure can rarely undo previous successes. The odds are far more in favour of it being galvanising for the next challenge.

Take Google. As prosperous a company as it is, not every product they have released has been a runaway success. Google Wave (software for real-time collaborative editing online) was announced with a dazzling demonstration at the Google I/O developer conference in May 2009, and began life amidst widespread hype. By 30 September 2009, when invitations to use the service were first released, the industry was hysterically aroused, with Google advertising it as offering a "radically different kind of communication".[9]

Reality, however, didn't match the expectations. Wave was soon seen as an expensive and dramatic failure. The product was so poorly defined and badly sold to the public that very few people understood its purpose or how it would add value to their lives. On 4 August, 2010 the project was killed, with Urs Hölzle, senior vice-president of operations at Google, posting a blog saying, "we don't plan to continue developing Wave as a standalone product". At the end of the post he added:

> *"Wave has taught us a lot, and we are proud of the team for the ways in which they have pushed the boundaries of computer science. We are excited about what they will develop next as we continue to create innovations with the potential to advance technology and the wider web."*

As Wave's plug was pulled, the tech press took wry delight in commenting on the failure. Crucially, though, it was a failure that Google quickly turned into value. Much of the learning from Wave's development went into their social network Google+ and core parts of the code were released as open source for customers and partners to continue innovating. As a company, Google knows that, to drive breakthroughs in computer science and the power of technology, risks have to be taken. And they can be taken without causing irreparable damage: Wave was a conclusive and public

---

9   Google official blog. *Update on Wave.* **googleblog.blogspot.co.uk/2010/08/ update-on-google-wave.html**

failure for Google, but it didn't stop us from continuing to use its search engine.

Fear of failure also stems from not wanting to intrude on a fantasy. Fantasies can carry a tremendous amount of hope, but they can also be kept forever at arm's length, somewhere we can mentally retreat. A fantasy can even be something we use to justify being miserable or unfulfilled right now because we haven't got round to it yet.

Fantasy has an intoxicating hold. Fear of pursuing something, on the chance it won't live up to everything we hoped for, is frequently disabling. Nevertheless, it's only a decision on our part that keeps it that way: all sidetracking can be turned to our advantage in time. *Monsters* wasn't Gareth Edwards' first film. After graduating with a short film he believed would have Hollywood calling straight away, he got deflected into a decade-long career in visual effects. But that time spent learning an industry meant he was able to make *Monsters* the way he did, with the budget that he had.

Crucially, he never stopped reminding himself what he really wanted to achieve or where his passions lay.

Negotiating failure can simply come down to timing. Jack Dorsey had the idea for Twitter in the year 2000, but it was the wrong time and the technology didn't hold up, so he shelved it. Dorsey only returned to it six years later while working at podcast company Odeo, with Evan Williams and Biz Stone, and that's when it worked out. Twitter now has over 500 million users.

We have a tendency to look at failure in far too binary a fashion. Failure is not the opposite of success, even when the outcome couldn't seem any worse. In her speech to the graduating students of Harvard University in 2008, J. K. Rowling told the story of how her *Harry Potter* books came about at a point she described as "rock bottom":

"Failure meant a stripping away of the inessential. I stopped pretending to myself that I was anything other than what I was, and began to direct all my energy into finishing the only work that mattered to me. Had I really succeeded at anything else, I might never have found the determination to succeed in the one arena where I believed I truly belonged. I was set free.

"Some failure in life is inevitable. It is impossible to live without failing at something, unless you live so cautiously that you might as well not have lived at all. In which case, you fail by default."

From the Wright Brothers to Google to Rowling, success has at points eluded them all. However, they each demonstrate that being creative and entrepreneurial is better served by not lingering on a downfall, but rather by learning to change course and apply talents elsewhere.

It is not uncommon for entrepreneurs to alter their business models if market dynamics change. Nokia, for example, began life in the 1800s as a Finnish paper mill. The company later merged with a rubber factory and a cable works to evolve – in the fullness of time – into the Nokia we know today.

Similarly, 3M (which stands for Minnesota Minerals and Mining), was founded originally as a mining venture. However, it was promptly forced to adapt its business model when output from its mine had little commercial value. Instead, it focused on creating sandpaper products, and in turn built a manufacturing powerhouse that came to be worth billions. Today they produce everything from Post-it notes to pocket projectors.

Adam Bird is a director and senior partner at McKinsey & Company. Leading both the Media & Entertainment Practice in

Europe, the Middle East and Africa, and the Digital Marketing group in Europe, he advises top management of media, entertainment, leisure and consumer goods companies. Adam is also a Young Global Leader with the World Economic Forum.

ADAM BIRD: *I think there's something that we have to think about as to how we are wired as humans. There's a reason we call it the comfort zone, because it feels good. And that's partly because of the way our brains are wired. Our brains are very complex, but they also want to operate at maximum efficiency. It can do a lot more, our brain, but generally we stick with what we know.*

And that drives an enormous amount of the way organisations actually operate. We have orthodoxies in organisations and received wisdom that give us comfort and reassures us. It is fundamentally at tension with creativity. I think the jolt that we have to give our brains to be creative is similar to the jolt you have to give to an organisation.

Failure is part of innovation and creativity, but I really don't like the word failure. It's got such awful connotations, and you hear it out there: "Fail Fast!" "Fail heroically!" I think what we like to talk about a little more at McKinsey, is experimentation. Experimentation has much more positive connotations, and we think it is absolutely essential to any sort of creativity or innovation.

Inherent in experimentation is failure. If you think about venture capital, for example, 15% of investments typically make 90% of the returns. That's a lot of failure, but it's also a lot of experimentation.

The issue is, how do you encourage that experimentation? How do you get people to move again and again beyond that comfort zone? And how do you generate the ability to do that within a company? Not just as a one-off, but in a replicable and scaled manner. We believe that creativity is something that anybody can do. Anybody can be creative. We fundamentally believe that, and I serve an industry where people think that only very few can. The blessed.

There's a couple of things that we would point to that spark creativity.

One of the things we would highlight would be explicitly overcoming orthodoxies. If you look at companies that have been incredibly successful, they have gone against some received wisdom. Everybody thought the Apple retail stores would be an absolute failure. The received wisdom was that having a high-touch environment for consumer electronics would never work. They went completely against it. They revolutionised the way the store was delivered. Everyone said, "You can have that, but it's never going to be profitable." The single most profitable retailer in the world on a per square foot basis is Apple. The second is Tiffany's. That ability to say, "We're going to go completely against the grain, we see an angle and we're going to challenge the orthodoxies" – not only is it a phenomenal experience, but it's also phenomenally profitable too.

The second thing we would highlight is creating associations. What we mean by associations is being able to pull in different bits of data or different observations from personal experiences, or thinking more broadly than what you know. Creating those associations leads to a lot of creativity.

What's interesting is that the more expert somebody is on something, the harder it is for them to make those associations. When we're trying to inspire our clients to do this, you would say, "OK, so you have a lot of data – let's do an exercise where we ask, 'How would Google manage your data?' or 'How would Disney manage your customer experience?' or 'How would Zara redo your supply chain?' That notion of analogies and stretching you out of your expert positioning or expert way of thinking is extremely powerful.

If you spend time with any venture capitalists, they will always tell you that they are not just betting on ideas, they are betting on people. The people who are curious, who perhaps have failed before, but ultimately have learned from that failure are the ones that they feel most comfortable about. It's not failure for failure's sake. They're actually learning from it.

There's a company called W. L. Gore, makers of Gore-Tex. What they'll do is actually highlight people who have tried something bold, even when it didn't work out. They recognise that they tried it. The message that they are giving is that it's OK – but make sure we really draw the lessons from it. Because what's worse than failure, is failure without learning.

Really creative companies are transparent about the creative process. They create a culture and a mindset that you should stretch your boundaries. They don't reward failure, but they provide the means to learn from it, so that the next time you do something, you're going to be better.

Industrial designer Sir James Dyson said, "I made 5,127 prototypes of my vacuum cleaner before I got it right. There were 5,126 failures. But I learned from each one. That's how I came up with a solution."[10]

Dyson's idea for a bag-less vacuum cleaner turned out to be one of the greatest success stories of innovation. But getting the idea was the easy part. It's the same with any success story worth our time. Creativity is not just coming up with an idea, but being able to stick with a problem long enough to come to a solution, without settling for mediocrity.

---

10   *Fast Company* interview with Sir James Dyson. 'Failure doesn't suck'. **www.fastcompany.com/59549/failure-doesnt-suck**

Putting ideas into practice requires stubborn resolve. This is where many people fall short. The people who can cope with the unease of not having an answer for the longest amount of time – these are the people who run companies, publish novels and ship products. The people who can weather constant internal dread and yet remain disciplined enough to make 5,127 iterations, knowing it will, at some point, turn perfect – these are the ones who turn whole industries on their head.

The value in this behaviour is not needlessly postponing decision-making; it is having the mental resilience to persist at something until it is complete to the best of our ability. Cultivating this way of thinking in every creative pursuit will mean we come out winning in most situations.

Academy Awards and mechanical trousers

An interesting story at this point is that of Nick Park, creator of Wallace & Gromit and four-time Academy Award-winner.

After graduating from the National Film and Television School (NFTS) in 1985, Nick was hired full-time by the founders of Aardman Animations, Peter Lord and David Sproxton. There, while working on commercial projects which included the iconic music video for Peter Gabriel's 'Sledgehammer', he was also completing his first short film *A Grand Day Out* (1989).

Each of his Wallace & Gromit films have been honoured with a BAFTA, received critical acclaim and outstanding TV ratings or box office takings. This has made Nick one of the most decorated filmmakers in the industry and universally respected for his craft. He is also one of the most gentlemanly and humble.

NICK PARK: *Animation for me started when I discovered that my mum's old 8mm home movie camera could take single frames. I already had an inkling that I wanted to do animation. I'd seen films about Disney and I loved drawing cartoons, so the two came together. It was a bit like thinking, 'One day, I might play for England', or something like that. I just thought if I keep going, keep doing, maybe one day people will know my characters.*

Production for *A Grand Day Out* began on his course at NFTS and was later taken on by Aardman. At the Oscars in 1990, the film was one of two short animated films nominated that were directed by Nick. The other, *Creature Comforts* (1989), was the eventual winner on the night. In total, *A Grand Day Out* – the 24-minute stop-motion film with characters made entirely from plasticine – took him a painstaking seven years to complete.

NICK PARK: *It was gruelling. It wasn't a straight road at all. After about a year or two, I realised I'd bitten off far more than I could chew. And I didn't have time to finish it, either.*

Back then, animation was a very solitary process at film school. I had to learn all these other skills. Eventually I just ran out of money and time, and then Aardman helped me. When I came to Aardman, that's when there was a more practical approach. They said, "This story is going to take you another nine years to complete." So it was a case of sitting down and thinking about how I could round it off. I had to do a lot of curtailing of the script. It wasn't planned. I strayed from the script enormously. I didn't know anything about discipline or structure then.

What kept me going was the knowledge or feeling I had that I was doing something different, creating something I hadn't seen before. I had been trying to think what to do for my graduation film, and I still wasn't sold on model animation. I happened upon my chosen technique myself really; I just thought I'd try this story out in clay before anything else. I remember doing a test of Gromit and just moving the eyebrows, and the effect it had on people.

For me, the most difficult aspect of filmmaking is the long-haul nature of it. Especially a feature film. The writing alone takes around two years. You think of a joke, and then four years later you wonder, 'Is it still funny?'

I guess it's a purifying process. The great jokes stay in, and you're slowly taking out the bad ones. And they are hard to let go. As Oscar Wilde said, "You have to murder your own darlings", and that's the hardest thing.

But there's something very satisfying about making sure it's a good story and a good journey for the audience to sit through. I just like thinking up original jokes and I can't wait to show them. And that keeps me going.

Nick's characters have enjoyed a prolonged run of success, with no obvious falter – whether starring in hit films or as the face of the Wallace & Gromit Foundation, a charity that helps hundreds of thousands of sick children and their families every year. And yet Nick still shares the same uncertainty familiar to us all ...

NICK PARK: *I'm terrible at going through doubt, partly because I'm very self-critical. I'm going through a strange battle at the moment at trying to find the right level. I think I'm naturally a perfectionist, but perfectionism can stifle creativity. The beauty of our kind of animation is that it's imperfect. It's never one or the other, though. It's a dance between them. It's a struggle.*

A friend of mine put it well: like any artist, you have to tame the materials you're working with. You've got to fight them and control them, and find the 'thing' in the clay—you've got to get some excellence out of it that wasn't there at the beginning. But at the same time, you've got to have a humility towards the material that allows the material to be itself.

I think it's just finding the right balance in that struggle. It can be difficult. At the end of each film I've made, after the mix, everyone is working so intensely on every edit and sound-effect and everyone is so serious. Meanwhile I'm thinking, 'I'm not sure if this is funny. What if the audience hate it?'

It's difficult, because I feel so lucky to be where I am. I didn't plan it. I don't tend to plan much. I just follow my nose. It's been good for me being under this umbrella at Aardman. I hate speaking high and mighty as if I know anything; I don't really. I think it's just important to do it. I've had a lot of opportunities to try and demonstrate that. And it hasn't happened over night; it's been a lot of hard work. You've got to be driven by some hunger to do something. And I've always felt hungry.

In 1999, Aardman struck a five-film distribution deal with American movie studio DreamWorks. The new partnership, a huge achievement for Aardman and one of the biggest deals to be achieved by any British studio, tied them exclusively to DreamWorks for their animated feature productions (the deal would eventually be cancelled two films early in 2006). Founded by Steven Spielberg, Jeffrey Katzenberg and David Geffen (the initials of whose surnames form the 'SKG' on the DreamWorks logo), DreamWorks Animation has to-date released 27 animated features including *Shrek* (2001), *How to Train Your Dragon* (2010) and *Madagascar* (2005). The deal meant Aardman could tell stories with radically increased budgets.

The first film, *Chicken Run* (2000), directed by Nick Park and Peter Lord, had a budget of $45,000,000. The two previous films Nick had directed were reportedly budgeted at £1,300,000 and £650,000 respectively.

The hunger that drives Nick, that drives any creative, can be easily tripped up by one of the most infamous excuses: lack of resources – whatever we think we need to make an idea a reality, the alignment of stars we mislead ourselves into deeming necessary. It could be access to a particular individual, a company, a skill or piece of technology. But more often than not, it's money. All of these things turn hunger into malnourishment, a very different – and a very debilitating – position to be in creatively. And one that needn't exist.

NICK PARK: *You never, ever feel like there's tons of money to play with. It just goes up more because you have to do more, or there's more story to tell. Even now, after all the success, we have to think how can we write more economically. 'How can we make this for this budget?' It is always a struggle, there has never been an open purse to do what we want. Even in the pre-recession days with DreamWorks, it was always a case of, 'How can we get this done for as little money as possible?'*

Jeffrey Katzenberg used to say, "Pick out your five money scenes, and don't spend any money on the bits in between!"

There's always a belief, both within Aardman and myself, that creative solutions often come from being forced to think economically. I know you need some money for some things, but as young artists we can be so set in our ways of thinking. We have a great idea that seems unachievable and we want to blame it on the world outside. Really what we need to do is look inside, check our own ideas; can they be done differently? You've got to constantly think on your feet, and more so as you get older.

There's a child within us all I think, and I never want to let that go. I just want to have fun. And this gets more challenging the more you do. I find filmmaking is very disciplined. Perhaps too disciplined sometimes. Now I feel like I'm learning an awful lot more about story and structure and how to put ideas together. When I was younger I didn't know that, so I would think, 'Oh, I've got this penguin, and these techno-trousers, how can they be in the same story?' 'But what is important is hanging on to that original something you have when you're young that is brave and not thought-through. The older you get, the more you think about things – but what's important is constantly trying to get back. That's where creative energy comes from.

I still look at The Wrong Trousers *(1993) as a momentous film. It had a massive impact. It just seemed to work. When I make another* Wallace & Gromit *film, I want to get back to that as a formula. The simplicity. Finding that original take. I believe it shouldn't take much effort, but somehow it does. I guess people don't see the effort – and they shouldn't. Michael Arndt, the writer of* Toy Story 3 *(2010), says that writing a screenplay is like climbing a mountain. But the first job is finding the mountain.*

Yes, you do need some money for ideas, but what people have at their disposal now with laptops and editing software and digital cameras and Canon whatever – you can just go out and do something. I could never afford sound when I was a kid, it was all on 8mm. Now if you've got it in you, you'll do it. You'll find a way.

Choosing a path

Like Nick, a lot of people tend to have a number of great creative ideas and possible paths in front of them. Do they choose to stick with their current job or start a new company on their own? Do they pursue this project over the other ten that they are interested in? Do they change industry and see where it takes them, or commit fully to where they are?

As a result, they can easily become paralysed by choice. Working our way strategically and wishfully through each outcome is compelling. So compelling that it's easy to forget the danger of not choosing anything at all. I have seen indecisiveness grind people and companies to a dead stop. And it's heartbreaking.

Constraints are typically regarded as a curse to creativity, but when choice brings progression to a standstill, we need to determine the absolute limit of when a choice has to be made, then *make one*. And at the very same moment, we have to drop any fear that we will be missing out on opportunities from the paths we didn't choose.

A useful strategy in product development for getting an idea off the ground is called the Minimum Viable Product (MVP). It can be applied far beyond products. The term was made popular by internet entrepreneur Eric Ries as a way to quickly market test a product in order to facilitate the most efficient and effective way of solving a problem.

A Minimum Viable Product consists only of the essential features required to put the idea into practice, and nothing more. The process is iterative and involves rounds of prototyping, presentation and analysis. It means investing a chunk of our time to pursue the idea, test quickly, learn, and then decide to whether to allocate additional resources to it, or shelve it until a later date. Translating our ideas into the most manageable undertaking possible – in order to get started – is an exceptionally useful, and often profitable, strategy.

While I was a partner at Zolmo, we spent four years of hard innovation to try and find answers in a volatile but lucrative industry that no one fully understood. Like movie studios, we adopted a model based on a high-risk hits business which required us to build premium products and content. It meant finding elite worldwide partners and talent, along with an understanding of leveraging celebrity, and in the process we collaborated with Creative Artists Agency (CAA) who represent two-thirds of Hollywood.

We pioneered with three payment models on mobile devices, two of which millions of consumers initially rejected. We were globally applauded for our hits, and at points had products that were complete loss-leaders. But we always dared to fail.

It is under no circumstances fun when things don't work out. You feel it not only financially, but physically. But not attempting something is even less fun, and a far less rewarding story to tell.

Creative potential comes from enjoying trying to succeed in the things we want to succeed at, whether or not we do. It means placing little emphasis on the outcome, and focusing only on getting the fire going. It's about leaving one less door with a mystery behind it.

It would be inhuman to not have any self-doubt, even though it's easy to see people at the top and beguile ourselves into thinking they have no fear of failure. They do. The point of tackling fear is not to try and remove it. It is an inherent part of life. We just have to be courageous enough to carry on in spite of it.

If you have an idea driven by passion that you are not sure you can achieve, do it anyway. If it doesn't work straight away, fight damn hard until it does. If it comes to a point where you have to walk away, remember – that is perfectly admirable. Just learn from it and keep moving forward.

Yes, there is a chance the idea might not work out. Alternatively, you might nail it and get everything you dreamed.

Be cavalier; dare to fail.

FINAL
THOUGHTS

Twenty-eight-year-old Californian-born athlete Alex Honnold is, without dispute, the most highly regarded free solo climber in the world. Free soloing is one of the most dangerous action sports imaginable, a form of elite rock climbing where the bold few who practise it choose to forego ropes, harnesses or protective equipment of any sort. They rely purely on their physical strength, their endurance and power of mind to see them to the summit.

There are no safety nets, no second chances. Nothing. With stakes so high, fewer than 1% of climbers attempt it.

In 2008, Honnold made a record-breaking free-solo climb up the northwest face of Half Dome, a towering 2,000-foot wall of granite in Yosemite National Park. The first ever technical ascent of Half Dome was in 1957 by a group of three distinguished climbers, Royal Robbins, Mike Sherrick, and Jerry Gallwas. As they plotted their route, they drove steel anchors into the rock, attaching their ropes to protect them should they fall. Their ascent lasted five days. Alex Honnold did it in two hours and 50 minutes.

Honnold took a legacy, a standard set by innovators before him, and was willing to fiercely exceed it. He put everything on the line, pushed human potential to the absolute limit, and in doing so set a whole different level of excellence. To Robbins and his team – the original pioneers of Half Dome – what he accomplished was unthinkable.

The world needs more Alex Honnolds.

AFTERWORD

Jamie Oliver
Chef and campaigner

As I write this at 36, it feels like only a moment ago that I was young and hungry like many of you guys are now. Even though a lot has changed since then, I still feel that the core of what I do – how I feel about it and what excites me – is the same as it was when I started out. Ten or 20 years from now I hope you feel the same way about your career. Sadly there's no one path to success, but I'll try to share a few of the things I've learned over the years with you. I hope some of these things will stay with you and prove useful or encouraging down the road.

The first and best bit of advice I can give you is to do what you love. Start by getting yourself into an area of industry you feel passionate about, and if you aren't able to do what you love during work hours, do it in your free time until the right job comes along. Before my career took off, I spent about 15% of my time working for free so I could improve my skills. I absolutely believe the right experiences and opportunities will find you if you do what you love.

Once you're doing what you love, there's a fine balance between being single-minded in your approach, and listening to the people close to you. This balance is impossible to bottle, but eventually you'll fine-tune your personal filter and find that sweet spot. Success, for me anyway, has always been about falling in love with great ideas and turning them into reality. There will always be people telling you your ideas won't work, or that you're going to ruin yourself financially (like my dad said when I set up Fifteen), but ultimately the ages between 18 to 30 are the best years for taking risks because you've got less to lose. Things might not work out, but even that's OK because failures shape you so you do better next time.

After years of working hard to prove myself, I hit 30 and finally felt like people trusted my judgement, which was wonderful for about six hours, until I realised that some people would run with my ideas even if they were totally rubbish. I guess what I'm trying to say is that the route to good ideas has something to do with staying true to your instincts, and also with having a great team of people to interrogate you, and to challenge and support your ideas. Be open to getting a bit of grief from them, because their questions will force you to defend yourself and think things through until you either spot weaknesses or polish those little seeds into things that really can work. If that team of people around you puts in as much hard work and passion as you, you'll always take those ideas far beyond your expectations. Some things are just meant to be. It's so important to make creative, rather than commercial, decisions. Your choices should never, ever just be about the money. If they are, things are bound to end in tears. Believe me, I know. When you follow your gut and make good creative decisions the rest of the details tend to fall into place.

This next one is really important. Regardless of whether you're a one-man band or a big business, the rules are pretty simple: screw people over and they'll never forget it. Be consistently good in your work and consistently good to people and they'll remember. Don't wait to be asked to do something, do more than expected and fix problems as soon as they occur. Behave this way right from the first day of your career and people will want to work with you. This work ethic will serve you so well because, once you reach 30, you won't want to spend another ten years making people believe they can trust you. By then you should be at a point where you're using the trust and respect you've earned to achieve bigger and better things. It's important that you evolve, and keep evolving.

A few years ago I used to meet the fashion designer Paul Smith for breakfast every six months. I really admired the way he ran his company and treated his staff, and I wanted to learn from him. For any of you who don't know, Paul is a wonderful designer who runs one of the most profitable fashion houses in Europe. He's also famed for being a nice guy and an absolute gentleman. His ability to spot talent and stick with things is second to none. At one of our meetings, he gave me a piece of advice that totally screwed with my head. He told me: never to try to be the best. Instead, try to be second best. Imagine hearing that at 26, when all you want to do is be the best! I didn't fully get it then, but I do now and it's been one of the most profound pieces of advice I've ever been given.

In the fashion world, being 'the best' might mean making suits out of gold that cost $60,000. Yes, those suits might be incredible, but how many people will actually be able to buy and wear them?

Compare that with seeing the joy and pride on some dude's face when he puts on his first beautifully cut 'off-the-peg' Paul Smith suit that looks and feels the business, and costs a fraction of the gold suit.

Being creative isn't necessarily about being the cleverest, the fastest, or the best. It certainly can be, but it can also be about surprising the general public with affordable luxury. The biggest rewards, personally and for your business, come when you can find ways of democratising that luxury experience or creative idea for the general public. Whether that's in the way you design a building, a laptop, a suit, or a meal, keep what you do real and street-level and work hard at getting to know the public because, whatever you do, they will always be your audience and will look after you as you grow.

I've learnt so much from people like Paul and the brilliant chefs I trained under. And as you go on your journey, doing whatever incredible things you're going to do, I hope you'll also have some empathy and respect for the young 'you's' out there. Devote a little chunk of your time to nurturing young talent coming up in whatever way you can. Don't fall into that playground culture of bad-mouthing people who happen to be doing something a bit cooler or cleverer than you are at that moment. That back-stabby culture is horrible and unhealthy and, to be honest, if you're a bitter, horrible person I don't care how good your product is – I won't want to buy it, or work with you.

So love what you do, take your work seriously, be true to your word, and be generous and charming to everyone you meet. No matter what you do, it's all about people, and inspiring them to believe in what you're doing. Do this and hopefully you'll find yourself with the career you're dreaming of. If you're lucky, that career will also pay you well one day. But most importantly it should allow you to enjoy what you do every day of your life. And surely that's the biggest reward of all?

Good luck on your journey.

Jamie Oliver

ACKNOWLEDGMENTS

To offer some context for what follows, I shall begin by saying that writing this book has been the single most difficult thing I have done in my career. Thankfully, *Spark for the Fire* exists for two reasons: diligent application of the ideas represented in each of its six chapters, and the people I am about to mention. To these people, I will add that my gratitude extends a great deal further than what I'm able to write here.

First and foremost, my parents Alan and Rita, and my sister Helen, who have continually taught me that anything is possible. They are always my main source of inspiration and have supported me without question my entire life. Needless to say, they are the experts on how to nurture creativity.

To my partner Stephanie, for somehow coping with me for two years while I worked on this project around my day job. I'm really not sure how she did that. Whenever I meandered, which was often, her words of optimism regularly put me back on course.

My friends Edward Shires, David Elwell, Ben Leavesley, Janet Wakefield, Dominic Burgess, Jamie Maule-Ffinch and Charlotte Smith who encouraged this book, agreed to read endless drafts or offered input. I have been accompanied by them throughout writing and they never once protested. Or at least they did it discreetly.

I owe special thanks to Harriman House, in particular Myles Hunt for listening when an exhausted creative director called, and to Chris Parker for his attentiveness and wisdom in the edit which has vastly improved every page. I will miss our conversations via the 'Comments' column.

To all the contributors who kindly offered their honest insights which have added the most value to this book. For me, they have also proved wrong those who say you should never meet your heroes. A special note of thanks to Jamie Oliver, as if he didn't have enough things to do, he still found the time to help. Similarly, to Ajaz Ahmed. Ajaz and I have known each other since 2007, and in that time he has been a truly great friend, mentor, and more recently my employer at AKQA. My career simply would not be where it is without him. Ajaz and Jamie, who rightly begin and end this book, are the two most inspiring people I have worked with.

Finally, my appreciation also goes to James Hilton, Louisa James, Anthony Finnerty, Ted Nash, the Art Directors Club, Rob Ford, Matt Booth and Michael Finnigan.

Let the next adventure begin.

*The six youthful principles for
unlocking creativity*

I

Embrace the Ridiculous

CREATIVITY FAVOURS INTUITION

2

Creativity is Transferable

EXPLORE, DREAM, DISCOVER

3
Beware Invisibility

YOU ARE ONLY AS GOOD AS YOUR ABILITY TO SELL YOURSELF

4

Curiosity and Purpose

SOLVE PROBLEMS THAT MAKE A DIFFERENCE

5

Learn Forever and Play

THERE IS NO FINISHED VERSION OF YOU

6

Dare to Fail

IMAGINATION IS ONLY THE
BEGINNING OF THE STORY

INDEX